The Art of God

The Art of God

Reflections on Music, Diversity, and the Beauty in You

Jimi Calhoun

Foreword by Paul Louis Metzger

CASCADE *Books* · Eugene, Oregon

THE ART OF GOD
Reflections on Music, Diversity, and the Beauty in You

Cascade Books
An Imprint of Wipf and Stock Publishers
199 W. 8th Ave., Suite 3
Eugene, OR 97401

www.wipfandstock.com

ISBN 13: 978-1-61097-423-3

Cataloguing-in-Publication Data

Calhoun, Jimi

    The art of God : reflections on music, diversity, and the beauty in you / Jimi Calhoun ; Foreword by Paul Louis Metzger.

    xviii + 144 p. ; 23 cm. Includes bibliographical references.

    ISBN 13: 978-1-61097-423-3

    1. Music—History and Criticism. 2. Reconciliation—Religious aspects—Christianity. 3. Race Relations—Religious aspects—Christianity. 4. Human Body—Religious aspects—Christianity. 5. Music—Religious aspects—Christianity. I. Metzger, Paul Louis. II. Title.

BT734.2 C24 2015

Manufactured in the U.S.A.   03/23/2015

In memory of William and Xanthyne Calhoun
and Jules and Lorraine Brown

Contents

Foreword

The great rock guitarist Jimi Hendrix strummed words together as he did his ingenious guitar solos. The following famous line attributed to him bears repeating, just like his songs: "Music doesn't lie. If there is something to be changed in this world, then it can only happen through music." If true, Hendrix was right, it would make sense to bring music to bear on such matters as race relations and religion. After all, we need to see change in our race relations across the land, and music was religion for Hendrix. Could the connection between music, race, and religion be one reason why we find a great majestic host from a multitude of diverse backgrounds singing to God together at the throne in the book of Revelation?

> I looked again. I saw a huge crowd, too huge to count. Everyone was there—all nations and tribes, all races and languages. And they were standing, dressed in white robes and waving palm branches, standing before the Throne and the Lamb and heartily singing:
>
> Salvation to our God on his Throne!
>
> Salvation to the Lamb!
>
> All who were standing around the Throne—Angels, Elders, Animals—fell on their faces before the Throne and worshiped God, singing:
>
> Oh, Yes!
>
> The blessing and glory and wisdom and thanksgiving, The honor and power and strength, To our God forever and ever and ever!
>
> Oh, Yes! (Revelation 7:9–12, *The Message*)

"Oh, Yes!" is right. I wonder what guitar riff Hendrix would have played to accompany these musical words!

The book you hold in your hand, *The Art of God*, is like a musical arrangement befitting these poetic and apocalyptic words disclosed in the Bible. For the author, musician, and Christian pastor Jimi Calhoun, biblical religion or spirituality is musical. God's diverse people sing a new song of deliverance and reconciliation in the kingdom of God. Pastor Jimi Calhoun's book is a creative and masterful exploration in showing how great music plays this role. For my brother Jimi, and for me, Christ's kingdom community, the church, can become great music, if we have the courage to move beyond uniformity and cacophony to symphony.

There are many good books out there that help us engage racial issues biblically, theologically, pastorally, sociologically, psychologically, and the like. But how often do you find a book that gets at the heart of racial divisions through music, which gets to the heart like so little else? This book about music and the heart will take you there. We need music to help uncover and heal our fears and hates that manifest themselves even now when we see youths wearing hoodies and watch the evening news about racial unrest in places like LA and Chicago and Ferguson, Missouri. May our homes, our churches, our city halls, and our cafes become concert halls where we address these emotions in grace and truth rather than harbor and hide them. Only then will we find transformation through the key change of God's transforming love.

Great music of whatever genre is not monotonous, but harmonious. Key changes that challenge and excite our imaginations and ring true to our hearts abound as effective improvisations. Melodious geniuses synthesize various musical forms in a manner that brings about new disclosures of God, our humanity, and our world. Such disclosures make possible new ways to live and flourish. Musical masterpieces do not ignore the human tragedy and evil, but include its notes in redemptive tension that climax in the explosive hope of transformation.

Jimi's music-history guide shows us how radically disarming and liberating music can be. Listen to the following words: "Music was crossing racial boundaries long before physical bodies followed suit. Music is spiritual, meaning it speaks to the mind, heart, and soul. It may very well be that because music is a multisensory medium, it does not really break down barriers as much as it blows right past them."[1] Oh, Yes!

1. See below, 108.

In the Bible, we find Jesus making music that blows right past our barriers. We can follow the Bible's lead of making music that reconciles and heals wounds of division as we play Christ's new song. In the pages that follow, you will learn how to play better harmony score after score as you accompany Pastor Jimi on his mystery tour through music. In response, let's all learn to sing together. As we sing, we will see that we are more beautiful together as God's masterpiece.

—Paul Louis Metzger, PhD
Professor of Christian Theology & Theology of Culture,
Multnomah Biblical Seminary, Portland, OR

Acknowledgments

This book could not have been written without the loving support of the following people:

My wife, Julaine Calhoun, my best friend and partner in everything I do.

My Family: William Calhoun II, William Calhoun III, Will Calhoun, James D Calhoun. Omari Calhoun, Xanthyne Calhoun, Gabrielle Boles, Marjorie Highshaw, Sarah Lawrence, Amelia Grider, Keith Lawrence, Rachel Lawrence, Leonard Brown, David and Susan Contreras, the Brown family.

My Musical Family: Leon Patillo, Dennis Marcellino, Neil Stallings, Carol Stallings Holt, Joseph Provost, Cynthia Robinson, Jerry Martini, Greg Errico, Clifford Coulter, Jerry and Annie Perez, Ron E Beck, Barry E. Smith, Lenny Goldsmith, Kaleo Larson, Victor Behm, Mario Medious, Malcom Rebennack, Danny and Debi Brooks, Eddie Tuduri, Dennis Kenmore, the Ingrams, and Cholly Bassoline.

My Spiritual Family: Zac Nazarian; Ralph Moore; Margie Waldo Simon; Scott Varneau; Kenneth and Lorraine Hoffman; Tim, Jenn, David, and Rebecca Hoffman; Nancy Mustard; David and LeAnn Bell; Glenn and Debbie Burris; Ted Brooks; Bill and Marcia Gross; Alan Kisaka; and Sekou Rubadiri; the Grables; the Selvas; the Daggs; Connie Jones.

My Family of Friends: Robert, Kimberly, and Ian Watson-Hemphill; Francois and Anh Gordon and family; Jose and Evette Hernandez and family; the Stroud Family; Stanley and Maureen Ermauv and family; Bryan and Blair Anderson; Sterling and Janie Spell; Nancy and Jim, Rudy and Leanne Green; Rich Miller; Michael and Samantha Lawrence; Mary K. Shanahan; Harish Kotecha; Mikail Davenport; Gavin Lance Garcia; Donny and Nicole

Christianson; Wayne Rediker; Mike Goodman; the Doyals; Travis. T.; and Becky T.

Introduction

A Note to You

Iask that you take an imaginary trip with me to a different time, to the
year 1947. The world at that time was a very different place, both in the
historical sense, and at a spiritual level. The Western world was recovering
from a global conflict that had caused millions upon millions of lives to be
lost. Adolf Hitler's treatment of Jewish people had exposed the horrors that
racial intolerance will eventually produce when allowed to go unchecked.
That said, it is helpful to remember that even during those darkest of dark
days, people were still experiencing progress and hope. On January 2, 1947,
Mahatma Gandhi led a march for peace beginning in East Bengali to protest
British rule over India. Gandhi's nonviolent approach to injustice, coupled
with a global sensitivity to the inhumane treatment that oppressed groups
received during the war, set the stage for an African American named Jackie
Robinson to break the "color barrier" in American baseball. At that time the
United States was fighting a war for freedom around the world, but at home
legal restrictions against "race mixing" were in full effect. It is hard to imagine
today that the United States had laws preventing white and black people from
interacting socially, and quite often professionally, but that is just how it was.

In the fall of 1947 another noteworthy event took place. Chuck Yeager
was credited with being the first person to pilot an aircraft at a speed sufficient to break through another barrier: the sound barrier. For quite some
time people believed that if an object were to travel faster than the speed of
sound, it would automatically dis-*integrate*. Similarly, for quite some time

people believed that if we were to ever break down the various barriers that separated people, this would cause our society to dis-*integrate*.

This book is not written about disintegration; it is about integration. It is about the integration of melodies, rhythms, and chords, that when joined together make up music. It is also about the integration of marginalized peoples, such as those with disabilities, the racially different, and the culturally different, into all aspects of mainstream life. In the pages to follow you will read a lot about the audible sounds of music that are produced by human voices and musical instruments. However, you will also read about another type of sound. The sound that I am speaking of may be an inaudible one, but it is a very real just the same. It is the sound of love, and it is the sound of grace. Together they can form soundscapes that bring people together through mutual love and respect. These sounds are not produced by voices or by musical instruments but by the human heart. They are heard when people live in harmony with the earth and with the people that inhabit it. It is my hope that the ideas and concepts in this book are taken as signs that will point us in the direction of becoming a more loving people.

On a personal note, at one point in my life I was a professional bassist. I was extremely fortunate to have performed on stages or in recording studios, or both, with several Rock and Roll Hall of Famers. I have performed with Dr. John, P-Funk, Sly Stone, John Lennon, Etta James, and Rare Earth, among others. Today I am a writer and a pastor, and I have written this book with the heart of an artist and with the passion of a humanitarian. The music business gave me the opportunity to witness firsthand the various roles that music can occupy in society. I have witnessed the way music can inspire people to take action they had never dreamed possible. Music certainly inspires me. In fact part of the inspiration for this book came from the British rock band Coldplay. A few years back they recorded a song about sounds titled "The Speed of Sound."

I used to sing Coldplay's song quite often at this one church where I was employed. I would sing the opening lyric along with the church musicians: "How long 'til I get in?" But as I was singing those words with the congregation, I was really singing the following question in my soul, "How long 'til I get (fit) in?" That is because at the time I was one of a handful of blacks in a church of three thousand whites, and the church was located in the South. My hiring did not come with automatic acceptance from everyone, and my time there was difficult. However, I did leave that church thinking that the answer to the song's question was sooner rather than later. Author Charlie Peacock, an endorser of my previous book, *A*

Story of Rhythm and Grace: What the Church Can Learn from Rock and Roll about Healing the Racial Divide, said this: "Artists, *especially* musicians, have always led when it comes to bringing racially divided people together." I selected a musical motif to discuss inclusion because music does bring people together, and it also provides a shared sense of identity. Music often records and then retells the stories of people's lives. Those stories can be in a cultural context, generational context, or even in a spiritual one, but once those stories are put to music, they last forever.

This book is about art and music, but it is also about the reconciling of people groups that have traditionally viewed themselves as being too different to coexist. In musical vocabulary the blending of different notes together is called harmony. The word *harmony* could also be used to characterize a societal arrangement where each person feels included and welcome. In recent history the attempts to bring people from different ethnic backgrounds together has been met with opposition from both or, in many cases, all sides. This must change because continual clashing produces a discordant sound that is not harmonious or pleasant to anyone. I have written this book because I have a vision. I can actually see in my mind's eye a time when harmony among human beings will produce a sound of sweet music to the ears of all, as well as an ever-pleasing sound to the ears of God.

I am hopeful this book will encourage you to see yourself as one musical note waiting to be used in concert with others by the greatest musician to ever exist: God. The appreciation for different musical styles is not innate but developed. People are not born preferring their own culture's musical style or style of dress or even food, for that matter. Many developmental psychologists believe that human beings may begin life preferring singular nutritional sources, but they soon develop the ability to receive nutrients from a variety of sources. One who enjoys a variety of foods is called omnivorous. When a variety of foods are consumed, either at one meal, or throughout the day, it is called a balanced diet. Today a balanced diet is considered to be optimal for good physical health. I am convinced that developing the ability to enjoy a variety of types of people is optimal for good spiritual health too. Bringing people together is really about balancing the rights of one group with the rights of the other group for the good of the whole. Scientific philosopher Ervin Laszlo says this in a poem that introduces the first chapter of his book *Science and the Akashic Field*:

> Our separateness is an illusion; we [all] are interconnected parts of the whole.[2]

2. Laszlo, *Science and the Akashic Field*, 6.

1

Art and Culture

Picture that you and I have just exited a brand-new shiny black chauffeur-driven Rolls Royce limousine in the luxurious tourist destination of Monaco, Monte Carlo. We are dressed to the nines, but we remove our shoes and embark on a scenic stroll alongside a glistening white sandy beach. Our eyes take in the ornate buildings that adorn the mountainside to our left. The curve in the shoreline briefly draws our attention away from the exquisite hillside architecture and back to the bluish-green tint of the pristine sea. As we walk, the wind provides relief from the midday sun that is just beginning to raise the temperature. In fact, the weather is so pleasant that we decide to quicken our pace until our joyful skip had reached the level of a jog.

Were you able to follow that vignette? Were you able to get a feel for the action? If you just answered yes to those two questions, I would ask why. Allow me to answer my own question by putting forward a very unscientific theory. I believe that human beings think in images and pictures more so than in ideas and concepts. In the illustration above, written words evoke the images of pristine beaches and majestic buildings. When we listen to the lyrics of a song, they evoke pictures in our hearts and souls too. We do not simply "think" music; we think and feel it! When we read a gripping novel, or view a film that is done well, we do not just mentally absorb the story or plot. What we most likely do is enter into that story emotionally, allowing it to have a visceral effect in us, and tempering our own reasoned reaction to it. The phenomena I have just described could be called *visual thought* and *visual sound*. Art is one of the most powerful forces in our society. It is ubiquitous, and it wields an infinite amount of power and influence on most every person living today. Unlike the information we are able to access through modern technologies, art not only *informs* us, art *forms-in* us—it is able to influence a wide range of human emotions, beliefs, and attitudes as it *re-forms* us.

Let us pause here to establish a working definition for the word *art*. I acknowledge up front that a simple definition for a word that describes something so very subjective is tricky, but here it goes. Art is a vehicle used to express human thought and emotion via a plurality of forms. Merriam-Webster's dictionary defines the noun *pluralism* the following ways: "The quality or state of being plural—A theory that reality is composed of a plurality of entities."[1] Webster's defines the term in other ways as well, and we will come back to them later, but for now let us focus on just this one. It is the phrase "that reality is composed of" that is germane to our discussion because the phrase suggests that diversity is written into the DNA of all that exists. We need not look any further than art to discover evidence that my premise is on good footing. The arena of art includes music, poetry, sculpture, computer graphics, photography, baking, cooking, self-defense, creative writing, lowbrow street art such as pop surrealism, the more conventional type of art displayed in traditional galleries, as well as many other disciplines too numerous to list here. Art is diverse, and you can see that having a plurality of art options is actually a good thing. Most of us use and enjoy one or more of the art forms just listed.

Recently the word *diversity* has become more synonymous with engagement based on division (a negative) and less connected with pluralism, which is the acceptance of peaceful coexistence (a positive). Pluralism within the art world is what diversity should be to culture—an amalgam of different entities that produce coherence and compatibility. Allow me to suggest that the best way to view art is through the lens of this simple aphorism, "All is art, and art is all." Every art form may not be equally enjoyed by all, but all art is equal. Where there is art, there is beauty. Art is variegated in structure and yet similar aesthetically—art proves that compatibility can be achieved where differences exists. For this reason the beauty resident in each one of you makes this even more incredible about the art of God.

1. *Merriam-Webster*, s.v., "Pluralism," nos. 2, 4. Online: http://www.merriam-webster.com/dictionary/pluralism/.

The ideas and values expressed through art can teach us much if we are willing to view art as something more than simply entertainment. A cursory look at the history of art reveals that art has had a powerful effect on every culture throughout time. Common parlance might restrict the meaning of the word *power* to brute strength. The word *power* conjures up a picture of domination, force, or aggression. The power resident in art can occasionally be explosive, but it can also be gentle, even benevolent. An example of this can be found in a socially conscious song by U2 or in a poem lamenting the struggle of women worldwide. Art really does have a type of power all its own. It occupies a unique place in various cultures because its beauty has both intrinsic value and practical value. Art heals, it unites, it frees, it enlightens. Simply put, art has not only brought an incalculable amount of pleasure to billions of people; it has served a practical purpose by helping to shape who we are as human beings.

Socialization and Information

Let us take a look at some of the ways that art has been used in the Western world. According to a book titled *Art: A World History*, "art first manifested itself in Europe with the appearance of humans during the Upper Paleolithic Age (40,000—10,000 BCE) Motifs found in cave paintings and small sculptures from this time used the animal world for inspiration and are often interpreted as charms used to assist the hunt."[2] Immediately we see that art had a practical side in addition to adding beauty to its environment. Visual art told a story, and it also gave instruction on how to advance the number-one societal goal of the time: survival. This suggests that art added value to the lives of people, and it also recorded the story of those people that would survive thousands of years. It is worth noting that we would not know that our forebears organized themselves into communities and were hunter-gatherers if not for art. Allow me to push the envelope a little: If some communication systems did not yet exist (such as standardized spelling or vernacular speech), how did the people communicate with each other? Art! Art has been instrumental in the way that human beings have organized their societies throughout history, and that continues to be true to this day.

We will now take a brief pause from our historical journey in order to highlight one similarity between the prehistoric use of art and the way it is used in major cities all across America today. In many American cities

2. Buchholz et al., *Art: A World History*, 14.

new types of tribal communities have formed. Relative to art, the people within the tribe often interact with each other in a manner similar to the ways our ancestors did. These modern tribes are called street gangs. I realize that many view the American street gang as an undesirable subculture, but their use of art and symbol illustrates the continuing power of art. I do not want to debate what effect gangs have on our youth and the overall culture. I simply want us to see how visual art, in this case body art called the tattoo—is still functioning in much the same fashion as the visual art of times gone by. Visuals affect both what and how we think. I remember reading several years ago that a Greek philosopher named Aristotle said that a person never thinks without an image. That was not a direct quote, but today's use of body art seems to bear out Aristotle's basic theory.

A gang member in the U.S. will use ink to tattoo the body in order to express solidarity with that one group. The tattoo also enables the gang member to display his or her major achievements in order to improve social standing within the group. Gangs creatively use spray paint to place symbols called graffiti on buildings, freeway overpasses, and other surfaces, in much the same manner. Stone Age paintings were used all over Europe and North Africa by our ancestors. Graffiti, like the communication art form of wall painting from antiquity, is a crude and effective system designed to signal tribal unity and to warn adversaries to beware. My point is that art has always been used to communicate and record the cultural habits and history of every society. Art has also been utilized to broadcast the hardships and challenges of the people within societies, often having a unifying effect among the insiders. The graffiti on display in public spaces serve as a daily reminder of the harsh realities of life as viewed through the lens of a particular group. People in every society find it important to let others know that they lived and how they lived. Gang members want people outside the group to know their story too. Story is an extremely important method of transferring knowledge, both orally and visually, and there is no better way to tell a story than through art.

From Bridges to Basilicas

I was raised in the Protestant Christian tradition. There are many subsets within that tradition. In fact there are so many strands of Protestantism, each with their own unique expression of worship, that it can be difficult for people unfamiliar with the tradition to be able to view it as a loosely knit whole. As a younger person I knew very little about the Roman Catholic tradition. I knew that they did several things that were very different from the things we did in our church. The clergy dressed differently than ours, and there was a lot of ceremony with people executing certain body movements on cue. Their buildings were ornate in comparison to ours with lots of murals, statues, and figurines. And when I was a very young boy, some of the homilies at their services were in a strange language, Latin. However it is the statues, the stained-glass windows, and the other types of art on display in those churches that is of interest to our study of the history of art.

Many believe that cultures are formed when groups of people develop a common set of traditions, social norms, values, and customs. These things then become the ingredients that cultivate the worldview of the population. I would submit that it is also through the telling of stories that the attitudes, values, and the preferences of a group are cultivated, codified, and then passed down. The end result of this process is what we call culture. If you are a person that identifies with the Christian tradition, then the following observation may have extra meaning for you because we share a spiritual history with the Jewish people. It is nothing short of miraculous that the Jewish people have been able to maintain their cultural and spiritual integrity over thousands of years. They have accomplished this in spite of being geographically scattered, and despite suffering persecution at every stop along the way. How have the Jewish people maintained their cultural and spiritual integrity? Perhaps they have done so through the telling of their story, and then the retelling of their story, over and over again. It was through these stories that they were able to maintain their cultural identity regardless of the circumstance. Just as the Jewish people have passed their story along through oral and literary narratives, so the Roman Catholic Church has passed on its stories, theology, and devotion through art. Catholic Christians have used art to tell and retell "His Story," meaning the story of Jesus Christ. The result is that the Roman Catholic Church has been able to thrive in different places, and to adapt to a wide variety of cultural settings, all while maintaining its identity.

Europe attained the status of being the global cultural leader riding on the trails forged by the military conquests of the Roman legion, which ironically also facilitated the rapid spread of Christianity. The Roman Catholic Church became the face of this bourgeoning new faith in the West, and it was almost single-handedly responsible for Christianity becoming a major player religiously and politically. If the Roman military was indeed responsible for the rapid spread of Christianity worldwide, art was equally responsible for educating the new converts, and making this new religious form attractive. From the time that Roman Emperor Constantine converted to Christianity during the early portion of the fourth century, through the period referred to as the Renaissance, which many say ended in the seventeenth century, Christian art ruled!

The book referenced earlier, *Art: A World History*, is an excellent resource because it offers several pictures from this time period depicting the story of Christ and the teaching of the church. Perhaps you have seen some of the art from that period without actually being aware of its history. Have you ever seen any paintings of golden-haloed angels flying around a person, presumably God, seated on a lavishly decorated throne in the sky? What about paintings that depict Jesus on a cross, speaking to his disciples or to his mother, Mary, while he endures the brutal process of crucifixion? Through paintings, murals, and sculptures of biblical figures and Christian saints, nonliterate people in Europe came to grow in faith and knowledge. Think with me: Hundreds of years elapse; thousands of people—maybe more—were educated, trained, and nurtured in the Christian faith simply as a result of this one medium, *visual art*. That is a powerful testimony to the effect that art actually has on the society in which it is placed.

Art Comes Off the Wall

In 1439 CE Johannes Gutenberg became the first European to use movable type, and he is widely credited with inventing the printing press. I am aware that there were other people that laid claim to the invention, but this is a book about art; it is only important to point out that people acquired the capability to print books at this time. With the rise of the printing press and increasing literacy that accompanied it, visual art on church walls lost its role as the primary tool for transmitting theology and telling the story of Christ. The printing press allowed priests and scholars in various parts of Europe to study one another's work, thereby acquiring new perspectives on matters of faith and doctrine. People were now able to rapidly exchange ideas even though they were hundreds of miles apart. They could examine the teaching and the practices of the church, and then exchange notes on what they thought about what was occurring within the church. After several hundred years of relative sameness of faith practices within the church, the printing press forever changed the way that people lived out their faith.

The printing press not only allowed people to exchange ideas, it led to the dissemination of new ideas that would have a major impact on every area of the existing culture.

The term *orthodox*, as it is applied to Protestantism in the West, can be traced back to the time period approximately one hundred years following the advent of the printing press. This period in church history is called the Reformation. *Reformer* was a moniker used to describe a person who split away from the Roman Catholic Church, and then "reformed" a completely different type of church that continues to this day. In the hands of passionate and creative people, the one invention of the printing press birthed a new method of communicating with the masses, called tracts. These single-paged articles would give people that opposed the practices and positions of the Roman Catholic Church an instant platform to voice their dissent. In 1517, Martin Luther, a professor of theology at Wittenberg University in present-day Germany, posted on a church door a tract containing ninety-five theses. These relatively simple pamphlets set off a chain of events that altered the course of history, not only in Luther's native Germany, but throughout the world as well. The art of writing had now supplanted visual art as the art form most utilized within the church. It would soon cross over and begin to influence nonreligious people, including politicians on both sides of the Atlantic.

The Reformation brought with it a belief that Christ's story, and even church doctrine, could and should be taken directly to the people. Two hundred years after Martin Luther used the printed word to shake up all of Christendom, preachers such as Jonathan Edwards, George Whitefield, and the Wesley brothers were using the art of public speaking to reach the hearts and minds of millions. They capitalized on the opportunities made available by print technology. They wrote sermons and theological papers, and the like, and then read them to scores of thousands of illiterate people. Many historians record that George Whitefield developed his oratory skills to such a high level that crowds of ten to forty thousand people were able to hear his speeches at once, and this was at a time when amplification did not exist.

During the same time period that the spoken word was affecting Christian culture so positively, another residual effect stemming from the printing press was coming into prominence: prose. This was the time period when African chattel slavery was a hot-button topic in what became the United States. Brothers John and Charles Wesley and other Christian leaders were speaking out vociferously for slavery's rapid demise. A short while later the writings of some of America's Transcendentalist cultural observers—among them Ralph Waldo Emerson, and Henry David Thoreau—began to question whether or not the acceptance of slavery was consistent with American values. (They took up the mantle of criticizing their culture in much the same fashion that the prophets of old had done in the Hebrew Scriptures.) Both men believed strongly that slavery was wrong, but their shared beliefs did not translate to similar action. Emerson appears to have had a cautious attitude about the way those beliefs should be lived out. Thoreau, on the other hand, appears to have been willing to get actively involved in bringing slavery to a quick and abrupt end. However, both Emerson and Thoreau used the spoken word and the print medium to distribute a form of art that helped bring about change. They produced printed jeremiads on topics such as slavery, environmentalism, and the cruel treatment of America's indigenous peoples—all of which would reach thousands of readers. Their words also had an effect on America's politicians, all the way up to the president of the United States.

Art as Glue

What do presidents, kings, popes, Burger King employees, college students, migrant workers, and several million other people of every imaginable stripe and hue have in common? Art! People of every ethnicity and every social stratum have at one time or another enjoyed some type of art. They may have been inspired by it or touched by it in some unique manner, but art has had its effect some way and somehow. Recently I have been interested in the writings of Ken Wilbur and Erwin Laszlo on the subject of integral theory. My loose definition of *integral theory* would be the combining of several independent ideas, disciplines, and forms into one united or "whole-istic" entity. Think in terms of our Earth. It is home to a wide variety of "stuff," e.g., people, animals, vegetation, rocks, and water. Each unique entity is thought to be categorically different from the others, and yet they are all accepted as being part of what we call Earth. To this point I have been using the word *art* in a very whole-istic manner as well. We have looked at multipronged artistic disciplines that are accessed and created differently, but by my definition they are all part of a larger whole, or one category: Art.

This may or may not come as a shock to you, but human beings are often consistently inconsistent. To complicate matters even further, human beings appear to have some sort of built-in mechanism that drives them to study, master, and then attempt to control most everything that they come in contact with. One of the tools that we have developed to use in that process is the category. The process of categorical assignment typically occurs in the following way: We isolate a thing, we decide what it is and what it does, and then we assign it a category. That process works well when the thing being categorized is a static object such as a chair or a fishing rod. What happens when what we are dealing with is a dynamic system, such as a sporting event, a dining experience, a human being, or a work of art? Please allow me to once again answer my own question: the practice of assigning artistic endeavors to a single inflexible category is futile. Categories will inevitably break down. When categories break down, our opinions appear consistently inconsistent. Here is one example of what I am saying. Why do we call the sound that a bird makes with its mouth "singing," while we characterize the sound that a frog makes with its mouth as "croaking"? We draw a categorical distinction based on sound and not on process. Both sounds are produced by the mouth of the animal, are they not?

The first two books of the Bible tell the story of God involved in the process of creating. God creates plants, fish, plums, butterflies, spiders, dirt, and even human beings. The creation story may be the best example of integral theory that I can think of. The Bible specifically says that everything that God created within the system called Earth was "good"! This means that God was able to create one metacategory, to label all the parts of that category as good, even though the members of this metacategory were vastly different from one another in form and function. I will go out on a limb here and presume that the majority of us do not like snakes, scorpions, and mosquitoes. Imagine that we were all somehow forced to sit in a room and observe these creatures for a considerable amount of time, say several months. I would speculate further that most of us would never see any value, beauty, or usefulness in these particular creatures, no matter how long we studied them.

If we were then asked to speculate as to whether or not those creatures would make good or bad guests in our homes, we would probably answer bad. Yet the person responsible for creating each of them referred to them as good. Consider mosquitoes: they have a natural instinct to access the first available source for nutrition. However, when that food source is your left arm, a minor problem ensues. Because mosquitoes bite us to gain their nutrition, most of us will place mosquitoes in the bad category. Our disagreement with God about the goodness of mosquitoes may just be our perception. The reality may well be that the categories where we place most everything we encounter are primarily based on our subjective perceptions, which are arbitrary in nature and nothing more.

Why Music?

I would like to close out this chapter by discussing one other art form that can be very difficult to assign to a fixed category. In fact it may be the most difficult art form to categorize because it is both static and dynamic. I am speaking about the art form of music. We dance to music, we relax to music, we sing music, and we are passive recipients of music. The English composer Ralph Vaughan Williams said, "Music will enable you to see past the facts to the very essence of things in a way which science cannot do."[3] Music has the unique ability to cross every boundary that human beings create for themselves, and to transcend division. Author and musicologist Daniel J. Levitin addresses the same idea the following way: "Music is unusual among all human activities for both its *ubiquity* and its *antiquity*."[4] He goes on to say that "whenever human beings come together for any reason, music is there."[5] The Italian philosopher Boethius, who wrote in the sixth century, put it this way: "Music is so naturally united with us that we cannot be free from it even if we so desired."[6]

Have you not found the ubiquitous nature of music to be true? You go to church, and music is there; you attend a wedding, and music is there. You watch a movie or the evening news and music is there. Even when it becomes necessary to seek medical attention for something as discomforting as a severe toothache, music is usually there playing softly in the dentist's office. I am confident that I am on good footing to assert that the majority of people in the Western world live their lives against the backdrop of some type of music. The following chapters are designed to teach you a little music theory, a little social theory, and even a little history about the author. We can learn much from music, and from the lifestyles of the people who make it, about the spiritual elements of our humanness, so let's rock and roll.

3. Quoted in Horn, *Imperfect Harmony*, 88.

4. Levitin, *This Is Your Brain on Music*, 8.

5. Ibid., 9.

6. Quoted in O'Donnell, "Music and the Brain."

2

What Is That Sound?

I mentioned in the introduction that at one time I earned my living playing bass guitar in rock-and-roll bands. The fact is, I grew up with rock
and roll. It was the musical score for my formative years, and it had a
profound effect on my professional choices. I was born into a musical
family. My mother and brother were both excellent musicians. My early
interest in music was primarily in jazz. The reigning jazz king of the era,
John Coltrane, was my favorite musician. He was a major influence on
me musically and philosophically. That is, until one evening when I was
about to leave my home for a performance but lingered long enough to
watch the Rolling Stones on television. I was completely mesmerized by
their performance. It was not the song, and it was not the musicianship
that caught my attention. It was a "something" they had that cannot be
defined: it was intangible, and I was seduced. It was related to their sound,
but then it was not. Later I would come to understand that a certain feeling is transmitted when music is performed, which is not easily described.
It was their feel that was the attraction, and that feel was irresistible to me.
That one musical intersection led me away from playing jazz to a journey
down the streets of rock and roll. That trip would eventually lead to a spot
in the Doctor John Band.

Doctor John (aka Malcom "Mac" Rebennack) is a multiple-Grammy-
winning artist from New Orleans, Louisiana. I had the privilege of playing
bass with him off and on over a period of six years. The music that we

played during that time covered a wide variety of musical styles. When I first joined the band, our music was called voodoo rock. At that time Mac had developed a persona that was like a cross between a Mardi Gras tribal chief and a voodoo priest. Band members would dress in outrageous costumes as well. On some nights there would even be a live boa constrictor on stage with us. On calmer nights we would restrict ourselves to using a black pot large enough to conceal a petite female dancer. She would then emerge from the pot and dance with the band as we played.

When I reflect back on those days, it can bring a smile to my face for many reasons—not only because of the things we did as a musical entity, but also because of the effect that we had on the people around us. As if a snake were not intimidating enough, the cast of characters that Dr. John had assembled in his band was something to behold in its own right. There were a couple of musicians in and out of the band who wore eye patches similar to those you would expect to see in a pirate movie. We also had a guy who called himself Reverend Ether. He claimed to be a minister of "ethereal funk," whatever that was. At the beginning of our performances Dr. John would come onstage with a large satchel filled with glitter that he called "gris-gris" (pronounced "gree-gree"). The "medicinal properties" of the gris-gris that the good Doctor used were many—the main one being that it was purported to have the ability to cast spells of good fortune on people, and bring peace wherever it came to rest. For us it had a very high entertainment value, aside from any other consideration.

Consider, for instance, that you are a musician and you have just taken the stage dressed in a very colorful but hot costume. You know that shortly after you begin to play the opening number, Mac will make his entrance, and with that entrance comes his satchel of gris-gris. You are aware that in a matter of minutes you will be showered with the stuff. Not just you, I should add, but also anyone and everyone in Dr. John's path will be fair game, including the audience. Your hair, your clothing, your instrument, even your face are viable targets: nothing is off-limits. Yes, the glitter was messy and it seemed to stick to everything that it came into contact with. I assure you that it really took a lot of effort to wash that stuff out of one's hair. Many times there was enough gris-gris residue in our hair to get some very long stares from the other passengers on the plane the next day.

Our usual touring routine was to fly to a different city every day or two. We would then go to the venue for a short rehearsal called a sound check. Knowing what you now know about what comes out of Mac's satchel of gris-gris, you can appreciate that the first concern at sound check had little to do with sound. Actually, most of us attempted to guess which side of the stage Mac would enter from, and then fight for the staging area on the opposite side to avoid the gris-gris onslaught. Writing about this so many years later has caused me to realize something else. In most cities we would only play one night, and this meant that we never stopped long enough to consider how hard the cleanup crew must have had to work after we left. Sad that there are so many areas of life that are like that for most of us. We rarely stop and think about how our actions impact the lives of others. A similar thing happens in the form of lifestyle blindness, and it happens all too frequently in race relations.

Let me share another interesting incident that happened on one of our tours during the voodoo era. One of our shows almost did not happen because we were arguing with one of the other bands on the bill. In this instance, it happened to be the featured act, Alice Cooper. Alice Cooper is the person who introduced the world of rock and roll to the flamboyant stage theatrics that Kiss, Marylyn Manson, and Lady Gaga popularized later on. Alice used electric chairs, guillotines, and other props that most bands considered bizarre, including a boa constrictor like ours. The argument was the result of a disagreement about which band was going to use a snake in their show that night. Actually both bands had been employing a snake in their shows for quite some time, but it seems this night was the first time they had been booked on the same stage. Being that Alice was the headliner, Dr. John and our band and was scheduled to play first. Alice and company felt that our use of a snake prior to their performance would diminish the surprise effect of their using a snake. This resulted in a bunch of very large-egoed rock-and-roll peaceniks displaying their true values for all to see. We espoused an ethos of peace for others to live by, but we felt no compunction about fighting among ourselves. Living a lifestyle at odds with professed values is not limited to rockers and other celebrity types, is it? I suspect every segment of society is equally guilty to varying degrees, including churches and those involved in racial reconciliation.

Right Thing at the Right Time

Let us take a moment to review some of the history of rock and roll in order to help get a better understanding about why it has always been thought to be inherently rebellious. In 1955 rock and roll was not simply a different sound; it was a brand-new sound. The person mainly responsible for this new sound becoming a national phenomenon was a man named Alan Freed. Mr. Freed worked at an AM radio station in Cleveland, Ohio, playing recorded discs made from vinyl that spun at a speed of forty-five revolutions per minute. For those not familiar with forty-fives, they were black discs about one-and-a-half times the size of today's compact discs, and they each contained one song per side. The music was recorded on analog tape, transferred to a master tape, and then pressed onto the disc. For this reason, Alan Freed was known as a *disc jockey*. He was called this in part because of the discs from which he played music; but I suspect that another reason for the *jockey* moniker was his *riding* the program's playlist for the day. Riding the disc meant that the jockey would select what records to play, and then through the use of commentary would hype the artists between songs. This resulted in the disc jockey having complete control over what the listening audience would hear, and what musicians and bands, and what type of music, they would eventually come to like.

At that time the United States was coming out of a different war than the one referenced in the introduction. Technically it was called a "police action," and it was fought in Korea. Americans lived primarily in cities, and they spent most of their time in their ethnically homogenous neighborhoods. They listened to ethnically homogenous music as well. Radio programming either reflected the tastes of their listening audiences, or it influenced them. Disc jockeys either picked or played the music that they perceived their listeners preferred. Unfortunately, this meant that the musical genres given airtime on the radio were selected pretty much along geographic and racial lines.

Part of the genius of Alan Freed was that he recognized that the styles of music on the radio were not that different from one another in a musical sense. Mr. Freed decided that he would mix four uniquely American music styles together as part of his regular programming. He would play a country song (country music was considered a white genre), followed by a rhythm-and-blues song (rhythm-and-blues music was considered a black genre). Then he would play an American folk song (popular in the white community), followed by a pure blues song (popular in the black community). His daring new approach was met with confusion and fierce opposition, but he persevered. His perseverance paid off. When asked about his new format of hybrid music he called it "rock and roll." Mr. Freed's term altered the face of American music forever. This reworked title to a traditional folksong written in 1907 expresses some of the negative reaction that many had to this new sound: "Mama Don't Allow" ("don't allow no funky knuckle—rock and roll—music in here").[1] As rock and roll was becoming more popular it began to be viewed as a threat to all that was moral, pure, and purely white. This is why songs were written protesting the fact that many parents did not allow their kids to listen to any rock-and-roll music whatsoever.

Let us take a closer look at the way that the new sound was received by the less accepting people of the period. On September 9, 1956, a young singer named Elvis Presley appeared on a television program called *The Ed Sullivan Show*. True to the musical template established by Alan Freed, Elvis's music was a blend of country and rhythm-and-blues. Put another way, Elvis offered a blend of white and black musical styles. This revolutionary musical blend captured the imagination of the entire nation. There was one problem, and that was that Elvis's musical and performance style closely resembled those employed by the black musicians of the time. Adjectives typically reserved for black people (*vulgar, indecent,* and *disgraceful*) were used to describe Presley and the new sound of rock and roll in general. Many conservative groups staged boycotts of the stores that sold his records and of the stations that played them. They barraged the sponsors of the radio stations, television stations, even Elvis's own record company, with threatening, hateful letters. Some went so far as to burn Elvis's image in effigy.

Rock-and-roll music was soon viewed as a major threat to American values. People feared that the social order that they had grown accustomed to would soon become a thing of the past. There were many who feared that once the blending of "racially pure" musical styles became commonplace, then the kids who followed the music might actually start mixing. Their fears were well founded because that is precisely what happened. Alan Freed began promoting shows in which black entertainers and white entertainers performed before the same audience though not at the same time, and those shows attracted racially mixed audiences. White parents were outraged that this new musical sound had brought with it the possibility that young teenaged whites would actually dance with, and possibly even date, teens from other racial groups. Musical multiculturalism was well on its way to being a reality long before the conversation about societal multiculturalism even started.

1. Lyricsplayground.com/, "Mama Don't Allow," line 5.

I remember singing songs about the new beats of rock and roll, songs describing the reaction to these new sounds. I know that when we performed people clapped their hands and danced in the aisle and in their seats to every song. The one picture that has stayed with me through the years is that of happy dancers unable to "be still" when a rock-and-roll beat was being played. I share this because it is important to understand that even with all the controversy surrounding the birth of rock and roll, it was really only dance music. The music was created to make people happy—happiness came through dancing the stressors of the week away at parties, dance halls, and nightclubs. During the infancy of rock and roll, the intent of the performers was to perform songs about teen romance, hot-rod cars, and the rigors of high school. The clapping of hands and the stomping of feet was the goal of the music, and not social rebellion. A negative reaction to rock and roll by the conservative adults of the time period led to a counterreaction in the form of rebellious behavior by the youth. Not only was a new cultural art form named rock and roll born during this time, but through this music a new tool for voicing displeasure was born as well.

The Sound of Innocence Lost

If you could go back in time and listen to the lyrical content of the songs that elicited such a strong reaction by the average parent of the day, you would probably be asking yourself, what was the big deal? What follows is just a small sampling of song titles that sent some over the top: "Rock around the Clock," "Hound Dog" ("Rockin' All the Time") "Let the Good Times Roll," and finally "Everybody Let's Rock." One rationale used by some to explain their virulent reaction to these types of songs was that the word *rock* was a euphemism for sex, and so "rocking around the clock" was having sex around the clock. The same logic was also applied to the word *roll*. Really now—how many teenagers in the 1950s would have been out past 10 p.m. without a chaperone? I am told not too many. The other leg that the objectors to the new sounds of rock and roll stood on was the notion that the beat is too African and therefore of the devil.

As time passed, rock and roll became synonymous with youthful rebellion, and as we moved into the 1960s, that perspective eventually became a reality. The adults of the 1950s hounded the music into counterculture status, and the beatniks and hippies of the 1960s picked up the baton and ran with it. What the rock-and-roll music of the '60s became was not background for a new dance craze, or singing songs about teenaged heartbreak, but music containing serious social commentary. Artists like Bob Dylan and others were not writing songs about the fastest car at the beach, or someone's girlfriend denying him a goodnight kiss at the end of a date. The age of innocence had ended because the Elvis years showed musicians just how much power existed in their Fender guitars. They decided to take on social issues such as the Vietnam War, poor race relations, and the economic inequities that were the result of those poor race relations.

Poet Ralph Waldo Emerson was once commissioned to write a poem to honor American independence from Britain. That poem was soon put to music and sung on July 4, 1837. One of the stanzas in the poem mentioned a rifleshot that was heard around the world. The idea was that this shot by a lowly and meek farmer initiated what we call the Revolutionary War. Alan Freed fired a different type of shot heard around the world when he coined the term *rock and roll* to describe a new sound in music. Today a sound that was created for teenaged fun is used to critique many of the cultural ills that exist in our society. It is also being used to bring comfort and hope to people who are facing challenges in life. However, rock and roll is still an art form at its core. Like other art forms before it, rock and roll has become a vital component of what it is that makes us who we are as a culture, and for this I say, long live rock and roll!

3

A Rocker's Lot Is Not a Happy One

As I previously stated, from its inception rock and roll was used as a vehicle for partying. It was music that was used to dance and idle away time. However, it soon evolved into a serious art form that critiqued many of the shortcomings of its surrounding culture. Artists such as Bob Dylan, the Beatles, The Rolling Stones, Sly Stone, James Brown, and Jimi Hendrix were beginning to use their stature as rock's reigning royalty to sing about racism, poverty, the war in Vietnam, and other social ills that plagued the Western world during that time. The title of this chapter comes from a recollection that I have of a newspaper headline announcing the death of Jimi Hendrix. I have no idea why the author of the article chose the angle that Jimi's death was in some way related to unhappiness, but that certainly was the author's perspective. I want to use that headline that was birthed in tragedy of the past to illustrate some current problems in our society.

To be young, gifted, and rich is to live the lifestyle that a 1970s rock-and-roll star lived. It was one of fame, financial independence, and a considerable amount of freedom. Having the freedom to do as one pleased often led to a way of life that resulted in certain forms of excess. Some speculate that somewhere within the psyche of many high-profile artists exists a degree of insecurity and a bent toward self-destruction. They believe that this personality trait is fueled by a lack of preparedness for their sudden success. Perhaps this explains why the headline's author was able to reach the conclusion that Jimi Hendrix, who was at the peak of his success when he died, could be unhappy. Let me stop right now and be perfectly clear: I do not know anything about the death of Jimi Hendrix. I am using Jimi as a model—a metaphor if you wish—for thousands of other musicians, including myself. I can speak from personal experience that as stated in the title to this chapter that much of what happens to many rockers over their careers would not cause them to be a "happy lot." This is even truer if said happiness is linked to financial success, because for the vast majority there rarely was any. Musicians that see fame as the primary goal, and not the by-product of perfecting their craft, are rarely satisfied with either. Please understand that most musicians do not play music to be successful materially. The majority of rockers play their music because they are passionate about the art, and that is a different form of happiness. My personal theory about why so many rock stars use drugs and drink, only to then self-destruct, is not because of any failure in the marketplace. I believe that many of these stars feel a lack of acceptance for simply being ordinary human beings after achieving so much fame.

Try to imagine that your job required you to be "on" 24/7. Having to continually be the person that you are on stage—because that is exactly what many of your fans expect from you daily. The sad part is that eventually some of these very successful artists fall victim to becoming a mere caricature of their own created image because of the pressure to be "on" all the time. This results in the person that they were before the fame becoming completely lost. So many of the people around these artists seem reluctant to encourage them to change or develop themselves spiritually. Management often discourages them from growing as human beings because that could eventually lead to their money stream drying up. Here is an example of what one top-selling artist named Cat Stevens did to escape the cycle. At the height of his fame, he simply walked into his management's office one day and announced that he would not be playing rock and roll any longer. Apparently he had experienced a religious conversion and would now be devoting his time and talent to activities consistent with his faith. Many artists are keenly aware that their audiences expect them to remain as they began forever. Can you see how this might lead to an artist feeling trapped by the very world that she or he had worked so very hard to create? Fame is illusory, and it has no intrinsic value: it is probably true that the only value any of us have is that which is given to us by the master artist, God.

Out or In?

Gaining access *to* something is what most of us spend our lives attempting to achieve. We chase after the funds necessary to make "the best things in life" accessible. We are social beings, and that results in our having a desire to access love, respect, and approval from others. By necessity, each of those desires involves another person to be actualized. Love needs to be given by someone, and in our culture respect most often needs to be earned from someone. When those basic desires are withheld or denied, that results in a form of rejection. But what happens when the gatekeepers of love, respect, and approval decide to withhold those things based on nothing more than their perception of an individual's physical abilities? What happens when physical impairments signal to an entire society that people in that condition do not need, or do not deserve, to have those most basic of human desires fulfilled? The people I am referring to are those living among us who live with moderate or severe disabilities.

Before I tell you a couple stories, allow me to clarify terms. Have you ever considered how we use the word *reject*? I only use it to communicate the opposite of accepting or receiving something. To break it down even further, I only use the word when I want to send a delivery from UPS back, or when I disagree with something being said to me. Because of my limited usage of the word, I thought it best to research it before sharing it with you. What I discovered was very interesting. The online search engine Google also has its own dictionary. That dictionary had one definition that said this about the word *reject*: "a person or thing dismissed as inadequate as failing to meet one's standards or satisfy tastes." Our country has a very long history of dismissing people based on the majority's tastes and preferences. Through the tireless efforts of one of my musician friends, I learned to be sensitive to the lonely existence of a group of people that are not on the front burner of political or social action that often.

> "It is a beautiful truth that every human being contains some-
> thing of the artist in them."[1]
>
> —WALT WHITMAN

---

1. *Wikiquote.* "Walt Whitman," http://en.wikiquote.org/wiki/Walt_Whitman/.

Allow me to introduce you to Eddie Tuduri. Eddie is a longtime friend, a very talented drummer, and also a humanitarian. While in rehabilitation for a broken neck that he received in a surfing accident, Eddie discovered a way to use his musical background to help others overcome physical challenges. The name of the program that Eddie founded is the Rhythmic Arts Project. What started in a hospital bed with one individual has now branched out into an organization that helps kids around the world. The program utilizes drums and other percussion instruments to help people suffering from severe brain damage, autism, and other physical and mental challenges that preclude them from full participation in mainstream life. I heartily recommend that you look into the program online because they do amazing work.

A few years ago Eddie came to Austin, Texas, where I presently reside and asked that I assist him with some classes that he was about to teach. I accepted, and it was through this involvement that I became aware of a population that is often summarily rejected as though to reject them is the only natural thing to do. Our society's way of dealing with this group of people seems to travel along these tracks: these people are unable to be productive in society, therefore they do not deserve equal treatment. To be clear, I have never actually heard anyone say these exact words, but I have certainly felt the sentiment coming from far too many people. Eddie's population consists of children with severe cognitive or physical disabilities or both. The Rhythmic Arts Project exists to empower this people group by teaching them basic life skills in ways that they can easily grasp. Our culture frequently decides that the best thing to do with these kids is to warehouse them in a manner much like our prison population. The rejection that I have experienced throughout my life results from people making a judgment about me once they see my skin color, and so I understand the pain of not being invited in solely because of appearance. These wonderful kids suffer a similar form of rejection, even though many are not ever seen in public due to being institutionalized. There is an adage in our culture that says "out of sight, out of mind." Once I witnessed how this segment of our society is often treated, I knew the adage was all too true. Following that experience, I immediately began to look for ways to get to know people who were classified as "disabled" or as "people with disabilities."

The church where I was employed at the time had just begun an outward-focused emphasis. My colleague Bruce and I began to explore ways that we could serve people living on the margins of our society. One of the ideas that emerged was that we would stage concerts for the hearing impaired at a local school for the deaf. The plan was to bring in visual art such as paintings and sculptures into the school's auditorium. We would get some large bass speakers called subwoofers, sufficient in size to create vibrations that the students could feel. Then we would have the artist present their art sequentially in a manner that, in tandem with the vibrating pulse of the beat, would mimic a music concert for the hearing. The plan was to have volunteers from our church enjoy the concert with the students as spectators. The goal was more than simply providing entertainment for the students. We wanted the kids to have a meaningful interaction with people from the hearing world and vice versa. We knew these kids lived in a pretty isolated subculture, and we wanted some outside exposure for them. This led to my looking for other opportunities to serve others who were out of sight and out of mind. This search led to me to Chris.

The Refuge

Christine, who we call Chris, is a thirty-three-year-old female, and she is white. She is also a person that most would classify as someone who lives with only mild disabilities, to be mildly disabled. To be quite frank, I do not always find the English language to be the end-all as a means of communication. It can be sloppy and inconsistent. It often leaves room for multiple interpretations, and we know that words can take on different meanings to different people over time. For instance, what does the word *disabled* really mean anyway? Chris was born normal, but as the years passed, she developed a brain disorder. This resulted in her losing some of her motor skills as well as some of her brain function. See there I go with the word thing again! What does *normal* mean anyway? Chris's dad once remarked that Chris is probably more normal than many that we accept as normal, and I could not agree more.

Chris's dad is a musician, and her mom is also artistic. This double dose of artistic proclivity in her parents' genes did not skip a generation. I have been told that prior to her illness, Chris was a wonderful pianist with an enormous amount of potential. One of the side-effects of her illness is that she is not always able to control the movement of her limbs. Her hands often shake involuntarily, and she can occasionally lose balance when walking. One thing her debilitating illness could not take away from her though was her love for music. One example of the way a word like *disabled* can be misleading when describing a person like Chris is that although her limbs may prevent her from playing piano, they do not prevent her from singing. Yes Chris can sing, and sing well.

Chris is unable to live on her own, and so she lives in a type of assisted-living environment. Five days a week she spends her time at a facility called the Refuge, which provides arts-and-crafts experiences for people living with physical and cognitive impairments. The majority of people who attend the Refuge each day are unable to speak or ambulate. They sit in wheelchairs, or on their couches, and take part in putting puzzles together or watching television. Chris and her dad invited me to have lunch with them each Wednesday, and after a few months I decided to bring a guitar with me. I thought that the presence of a guitar could coax Chris into singing after lunch, and it did. Over time my friend Robert, who you will meet later, joined the party. When Chris's dad has time, he often grabs a guitar and joins in on the fun. Chris really loves music, she sings well, but like many musicians she is somewhat shy. There have been many times when we would take out the guitars only to find that Chris was not in the mood to sing. The fact that we did not want to continually show up without having something to do led to an expansion of our music program at the Refuge. Here is how that expansion happened.

The majority of the time that we visit Chris there is a man named Allen sitting in close proximity to her. Allen is actually much more disabled than Chris. The most noticeable part of his disability is that he is completely wheelchair bound. His limbs are somewhat crooked, and his little hands do not function very well. However he is always dressed in a stylish hat of some type each week. This is because the hats hide the scars from the many brain operations that Allen has undergone during his life. The first song we performed as a group was the song titled "Don't Worry, Be Happy." When Robert first introduced the song, I wondered whether or not the song was appropriate. I soon learned how naïve and uneducated I was in this environment. The assumption I carried with me about people with severe disabilities was, how can *these* people possibly be happy? My perspective was so limited that I felt that singing a lyric such as "Be happy!" would somehow remind folks at the Refuge that they could not ever be truly happy. I can say emphatically that the time I have spent with these wonderful people has proved that my assumption was quite wrong.

To lovingly serve people like my friends at the Refuge requires patience, gentleness, and the acceptance of the fact that we are really no different from them. Mick Jagger once sang that "we all need someone to lean on," and there may be no truer words written in this book. Irrespective of our abilities, or our station in life, we can do very little on our own. Why is it that most of us shy away from entering into relationships with people living with disabilities? For many, the natural response to an invitation to love someone like Chris is to recoil from it rather than to embrace it. Fear of having our conception of God challenged could be part of the reason we shy away from this group of people. It is true that constant contact with people in this community could lead one to the question, where are you (God) in their circumstances? That question is one that many would rather avoid, and so it may seem easier to simply avoid the people who might prompt the question. However, Jesus's life teaches us that loving people is never about us, that it is about the object of that love, the betterment of the other. Chris's dad sent me the following e-mail that highlights this truth in words that are far better than any that I would choose. He wrote:

> One of the most difficult things about being Chris's dad is to keep it from being about me. I am involved, of course, but it is her circumstances, her conditions, *her life*. I cannot help her unless and until *I can get out of the way*. In the way? I am talking about expectations a father has for his little girl. I am talking about the pain of seeing her have seizures and physical struggles. I am talking about the frustrations of seeing her fall short of perceived potentials. I am talking about the utter depression of joy, love, hope, achievement, communication and being within the limitations of her skin measured by how I understand those fundamental experiences. So, I have to make a list and tear it up or burn it or chew it up and expel it in my weak moments; in stronger times I take it up with God about how I live my life to be like Him.

He continued on to say,

> For her, I have to try to understand and process things as close as I can to the way I understand that she processes things. I have found numerous revelations in that; she is not so unfamiliar. There are those unmistakable genetic connections that make me know how or why she is reacting the way she is reacting from a very gut level. There are the connections forged by years of our relationship; her devotion to me just as or more relentless and powerful as my devotion to her. There are the connections forged by the force of her own unique character, which is quirky and beautiful and sublime—all at the same time. There is love. Love for her, love

with her that is all the more precious and important because of the way she is. In the moments that I realize her specialness then it is true for me as well. That revelation, I believe, is the hand of God.[2]

You Make My Heart Sing

One guest in particular, named Jesse, has helped me see the humanity, and the value, in every single person. In times past that understanding was not always automatic when I would come into contact with a person with disabilities. Jesse also taught me that most of us are susceptible to making huge errors if we judge someone too quickly. Jesse is severely deformed according to the typical view of what the human body should look like. He cannot move his legs, and extending his hand even a short distance is quite an accomplishment for him. He cannot speak either, although he does attempt to communicate through indecipherable groans on occasion. He is able to say a version of "mama," but the way he mouths the word makes it difficult to understand. The pattern of the interaction with the guests that Robert and I settled on was to spend time with Chris first, and then go around the room to play and sing for the others. I need to add that many of the guests are so severely brain damaged that we can never be sure if they are aware of our presence.

My personal pattern was to stop by Jesse's wheelchair and sing to him just before it was time for us to leave each week. There was just something about his steely blue eyes that seemed to draw me back to him over and over. On one occasion after many months of silent Wednesdays, Jesse actually spoke to me. I have had few experiences more gratifying than watching Jesse make the effort to reach out his badly deformed hand to me, and then speak to his friend, me! You see that is exactly what I believe that I am to him now, a friend. In fact, I would not be surprised if Jesse was not using the months of silence as an audition to see if I was really friendship material.

I feel so very honored to be friends with Jesse and the others at the Refuge. However, to become a friend to Jesse required that I resign myself to the reality that he would never be able to acknowledge my role in his life. He definitely lacks the means to reciprocate like what occurs in my other relationships. The reality is that most of the friendships we have are based on affinity or reciprocity. We all enjoy hanging out with people with whom we hold something in common. We also like to hang out with people whose

---

2. E-mail to the author on August 2, 2013.

friendship can in some way benefit one or both parties. That is fine. However it makes it difficult for people with disabilities like Jesse's to ever have a friend. This is because many people simply assume that people like Jesse have little to give back. I can confidently say to you that although this group is easily marginalized, neglected, and often forgotten, they have much to offer anyone willing to invest the time. The key word in the last sentence is *time*. That is because befriending people in this condition does require a time commitment, but the amount of joy one receives in return is immeasurable.

One day I arrived at the Refuge a little early, and I noticed that a woman named Sherri was missing. I asked the director, a woman named Carol, where Sherri was, to make sure that she was okay. It turned out that Sherri was ill and had been hospitalized. I would later learn that Carol, this wonderful woman, had spent her off hours visiting Sherri in the hospital each night after work. Carol is not simply a professional caregiver for these very special people; she is someone who actually cares.

Carol's job is to care for at least thirty special-needs people daily. Each one of those clients faces a different set of challenges in life. Carol's job is not easy, and it appears to me that it is very stressful. She is in constant motion as she watches each guest while simultaneously meeting the needs of the one in front of her. While she is working with one of the guests, you can observe her eyes darting about the room making sure that other guests do not injure themselves. As she updates me on Sherri's condition. I am thinking that this woman has just spent her entire day tirelessly responding to the needs of these wonderful people. Then during her off time she makes the decision to spend even more time meeting their needs. It seems Sherri had fallen out of her wheelchair. She was on the floor and helpless at her residence for quite some time before being found by the nurse on duty. Carol said that she went to the hospital because most of the guests do not have much support outside of their immediate families. She added that many of the relatives are not always available, and even when they are, their visits are infrequent.

Then Carol said something that touched a nerve: "Jimi, you have no idea how lonely these people are!"

She was certainly right, because through all of my days in ministry, I had never considered how lonely life must be for people like my friends at the Refuge. Carol's concern for Sherri taught me that caring for someone by meeting physical needs is different than caring about someone by meeting their social and spiritual needs by being there for them when they need it.

"Wherever you go you find people who are unloved, unwanted and uncared for."[3]

—Mother Teresa

Early in my career I worked at a church called Hope Chapel, in Hermosa Beach, California. This church had an extensive ministry to special-needs people. The church was so sensitive to the needs of people with disabilities that they spent a large sum of money to reconfigure the building in order to accommodate this special group. I was fortunate to witness the remodel happen, and I was also there to see the results. More and more special-needs people began attending each week. My close friend Scott Varneau was the director of that ministry, and another friend, named Gloria, was actively involved. Even though I was a pastor there, and I was keenly aware of what was happening with this group, I never once stopped to consider what their daily lives were like. I cannot remember ever considering the possibility that they may be lonely. I was quite comfortable believing that we were doing an excellent job of ministering to this population, and compared to a great number of churches we were. However, at a personal level, I was not. Additionally, I had never even considered that intentionally befriending "the other" might have been something that God wanted me to do.

Eddie Tuduri related a neat story on the phone a couple days ago. He said that he was speaking with someone who was curious about the Rhythmic Arts Project. Eddie gave him an overview of the program, and the person followed up by asking Eddie what he did for a living. Eddie said, "I include people." The answer was a little too oblique or indirect for the questioner, and he asked for some clarification about what "including people" actually meant. Eddie seized the opportunity to raise the person's awareness of the way people with disabilities are often dismissed in our society. Eddie related to the man that people with disabilities are often invisible to others, or avoided in public spaces. Eddie asked if his conversation partner could recall an instance when he had intentionally been cordial to a person with disabilities in a public space.

The response was, "I don't know if I ever have even offered a simple hello to one!" Eddie challenged him to try speaking to the next person with

3. Values.com/, http://www.values.com/inspirational-quotes/4121-Stay-Where-You-Are-Find-Yo/.

disabilities that he came in contact with, regardless of where the encounter happened. As you may have anticipated, the man did just as Eddie recommended, and it changed his life. Apparently the reaction of the person with disabilities to the able-bodied person's greeting made such an impression on the able-bodied man that he promised he would never again treat a disabled person as a nonperson by ignoring their presence in public spaces.

In a bit of irony I want to quote Oscar Wilde. Mr. Wilde wrote the following words in the preface to his classic work *A Picture of Dorian Gray*: "All Art is quite useless."[4] What I understand these words to mean is that art should not be thought of in a utilitarian manner because art lacks any practical function. To Oscar Wilde, art is just art; it may have beauty, but art cannot *do* anything on its own. The irony is that in many ways Mr. Wilde's take on art mirrors the way many view people with disabilities. Many people are of the opinion that they cannot "do" anything on their own and that in many respects they are useless. My recent involvement with the population of people with disabilities through my musical endeavors has taught me to see things quite differently.

I have learned that every piece of God's art, including people living with disabilities, has both beauty and value, regardless of its ability to do the things we value or not. Mr. Wilde may doubt that art has any usefulness aside from the enjoyment of the consumer, but I disagree. Through the Refuge I have come to know that God's art—the human kind—brings both beauty and value to the world simply because it exists. There is beauty and value in each human being whether or not it compares in form and function to others. I have played bass on recordings that were popular all over the world. I have played music for movie soundtracks that have brought pleasure to millions. However, there was a time in my life when my musical ability was not obvious to most of the people around me. But it was there all the time. Even though many are unaware of the beauty within people with disabilities, beauty is there, in them!

"Perseverance is not a long race; it is many short races one after another."[5]

—WALTER ELLIOTT

4. *Wikiquote*, s.v., "The Picture of Dorian Gray," preface, pt. 11, http://en.wikiquote.org/wiki/The_Picture_of_Dorian_Gray/.

5. *Wikiquote*, s.v., "Perseverance," line. 11, http://en.wikiquote.org/wiki/Perseverance/.

Earlier I spoke of my friend Jesse at the Refuge. I entered my relationship with Jesse with no guarantees of success. How could there be, because in this instance it is probable that no one could actually say what success would even look like. Week after week I went to Jesse's area. I would speak to him and make my guitar available for him to touch. I thought success had been achieved when he extended his hand upward attempting to strum the strings. Later I realized that his strumming the strings may have been one form of success, but a better indicator was soon to follow. When Jesse uttered the word "bye" as I left, I saw success with him in quite a different light. I saw that my year and a half of small and patient steps was necessary for me to develop a genuine love for Jesse. It also gave him ample time to develop enough love for me to make the necessary effort to speak. For him, that effort was considerable, but that is what friendship is all about.

Getting involved at the Refuge has taught me that it is my responsibility to see the beauty in each piece of God's art. That is often difficult for me, and I suppose it could be difficult for you too. It is easy for me to go to the beach and see a thunderous wave as a reflection of God's magnificence and artistic ability. But to see a person with limbs that do not function, that are crooked and contorted—that is another matter. Appreciating people as they are was something that I had to learn to do. The Refuge has helped me to learn that a person can develop an eye for a wide variety of God's artwork, provided the effort is made. When I broadened my definition of the word *beauty* to include people I once viewed as disfigured, I did not lose anything. On the contrary, I actually added new varieties of human characteristics to consider beautiful and enjoy. For that reason I know that it is possible to add to the number of people to view as beautiful, and that keeps me excited about the future.

From Serving to Loving

What I am about to say is not being said for shock value, even though I believe many of us could use a little jolt related to this subject. Let me describe what I do every week at the Refuge. It starts with driving about twenty miles, and what I see when arrive each week varies. Occasionally I open the door and I see a sweet soul in a wheelchair sitting very close to the door. He is unable to control the steady stream of drool from his mouth and my natural reaction is to be put off to a minor degree. On other occasions there is an odor present in the air resulting from some of the guests' diapers not being changed quickly enough. At other times some of the guests are moaning or letting out guttural shrieks similar to those you would expect to hear walking in an Amazon rainforest. This may sound hard to believe, or even crazy, but every time I open that door on Wednesday morning, I see each of the guests as the art of God in bodily form, regardless of their condition. I no longer serve them—I love them!

I must admit there were times when I had to fight the urge to ask God, "Where are you in these people's pain?" In tears I would think, "Why have you allowed this to happen to these innocent people?" I spent many hours pondering what purpose God had in mind to allow people into the world only to suffer. My friend Eddie once said to me that people who live with disabilities can help a person find God. Being that I was a pastor, he probably expected me to know what he meant. I did not, and my pride prevented me from asking him to explain. Later on an internationally known Roman Catholic priest named Henri Nouwen would help me better understand my friend's perspective. Henri Nouwen was at a point in his life when he desperately needed to hear from God. He wondered if he would hear, when he would hear, and how he would hear from God. He later wrote that he eventually did hear from God in a clear and distinct voice saying, "Go and live among the poor in spirit, and they will heal you."[6] Looking at Father Nouwen's background a little closer reveals that Eddie was right about it being possible to find God among the broken. Henri Nouwen was a professor at Harvard, one of America's most prestigious schools, and he gave it up to live and work among a community of brain-damaged people called L'Arche. Henri Nouwen began his search at the top, willingly moved to what most would describe as the bottom, and God met him there.

My limited experience with special-needs people had made me more inclined to believe that interaction with that population would bring with it more doubts than certainty about God. However, through the playing of a few simple rock songs on a guitar at the Refuge each week, and also through playing bass at another facility for special-needs people here in Austin, I have improved the lot in life for a group of people who so desperately need it. Even though I am what most people would describe as fully functioning, it does not follow that I am any more valuable than my friend Jesse, regardless of my occupation or social standing. Let us move on and see if we can draw a parallel between the many elements necessary for us to understand what makes us human, and the many elements that are needed to make music.

6. Nouwen, *In the Name of Jesus*, 22.

4

Do You Hear What I Hear?

What thought comes into your mind when you hear the word *music*? How would you describe music to a person who is unable to hear? If you were required to write a paper giving the reasons why you like a particular style of music what would you say? I am a musician, and would it surprise you to learn that those questions are difficult for me to answer in a clear and concise manner? They are. Typically what I have tended to do is overconceptualize what music is by using my own personal idealized subjective abstractions, instead of simply saying what music does to me. I can focus on the execution of a performance, and then I hear nothing else. At other times my emotions are carried away as I listen to the beauty of an exquisite arrangement. Still at other times I am in awe of the way a particular musician is able to take the same notes I have used all my life and create something far beyond my imagination. My point is that we all listen to music, but we listen in very different ways. Different people hear different parts within the same piece of music and then single out what they hear for attention. Said another way, most people can like some parts of a piece of music but can overlook and even dislike other parts. We all listen to music for different reasons and in different ways.

Analysis aside, it is in the hearing that we know music, and one way that I listen to music is internally. Many times during the day I have music playing "audibly" inside my brain. Weird? Not really. Have you ever sung a song to yourself without making a sound? Sure you have. We all have. That is what I mean when I say that I often have music playing inside my brain. Being a musician, I also have the ability to see music. This means that I can visualize playing my instrument, and that in my mind's ear can hear what it sounds like. This chapter assumes that many of you have no prior musical expertise, and so I will need to get a little technical. My purpose is to give you some basics about how music is put together. Hopefully this brief excursion into the world of music theory will give you a better understanding of what music is. This will also help you to better understand some of the analogies that I will draw from the world of music.

I have a friend named Mike Lawrence. Mike is a lawyer, a guitarist, and a humanitarian. Recently he asked that I help him teach disadvantaged kids about music, using guitars in a way that would allow the children to actually play the guitars themselves. I believed that there was an enormous amount of potential in what Mike had created. I suggested that we standardize it and then develop a program in order to give more kids access. The program that we are in the process of developing is called TOP. That is an acronym for the Open-tuning Project. I am extremely proud to be involved in this because kids are able to develop discipline and have fun playing guitars, all while learning values and life skills based on a musical foundation. Allow me to put forward one possible response to the question that opened this chapter. Borrowing the words *rhythm*, *melody*, and *harmony* from our TOP curriculum I was able to settle on one simple answer to what music is: "Music is an auditory performance art primarily composed of rhythm, melody, and harmony."

Throughout my years as a professional musician there existed a running joke among my fellow instrumentalists: "Are drummers really musicians?" Actually the joke was grounded in solid logic depending on the way one defines *music*. Some would argue that for there to be music a melody must exist. Since a drum does not produce a wide spectrum of tones, the creation of a melody by a drum is very difficult. If a drum does not produce melody, then it is not really a musical instrument. It should then follow that if a drum is not a musical instrument, the person playing a drum must not be a musician. Logical, right?

I grew up with a great drummer named Barry "Frosty" Smith. One day I decided to call him and put that hypothesis to the test. Frosty pointed out that some drummers, such as the late great Tony Williams, are composers who write songs that contain melodies. Frosty opined that Mr. Williams was proof that drummers should qualify as musicians. Then I remembered that there is a type of drum used in the music of many of the Caribbean Islands called a steel drum. This drum actually produces many of the same notes that make up the scales that create melodies. Taken together, these two facts would suggest that certain types of drums are in fact musical instruments. Logic would now have to give way to the possibility that drummers really are musicians too. Just when we were about to end the conversation, Frosty hit the nail on the head concerning what is really important. He said, "It really doesn't matter to me what term is used to describe drummers. I am a drummer, I know that I am an artist, and I'll settle for that!"

What an insightful choice of words, and they are absolutely relevant to this discussion. In this chapter we are discussing the essence of music and also what it means to be human. Drummers and bassists are not the glamour positions in the majority of rock bands. Those honors are typically reserved for lead singers, guitarists, and occasionally keyboardists. Once people create subsets within a category, the subsets are soon evaluated qualitatively and quantitatively. People consider how necessary they are, and what it is they are contributing. These become the criteria for legitimacy.

We follow the same pattern of logic prior to granting full personhood to certain segments of our society. If a human being lives with disabilities, lacks expertise in a vocation that we presently value, or is the wrong color, then their personhood is often denied. Are people living with disabilities persons? Yes! Are drummers musicians? Yes! Human beings are different from one another. And each band member or each set of band members plays a different instrument. But there is a unity and coherence in the difference that makes each part indispensable to the whole. Accepting the difference within is the beauty of art. Just look at music. Drums create rhythm, and rhythm is an essential element in music. Rhythm is also a separate art in and of itself. It is utilized in the art of dance, sport, public speaking, and other performance-oriented activities. Additionally, our lives are lived out in various patterns of rhythm, whether we are aware of them or not.

In order for melody to exist, a logical order to the placement of each note must be considered. An arrangement of pitches different from one another is not automatically a melody. These pitches, or frequencies, must be arranged in some type of sequence that adheres to the natural laws of music that we are about to discuss. Once the desired sequence of the notes is arrived at, it is then repeated. At this point the artist is using rhythm and pitch to create a melody, and a song is born. I cannot imagine a way that a melody can be constructed without some type of a rhythm pattern being involved. I also cannot envision a person going through life without developing some type of rhythm pattern to it. We may call it by a different name such as a habit, a routine, or a proclivity. When human beings engage in repetitious patterns of thought and behavior, this pattern is directly analogous to a rhythm. These repetitious thought patterns and behavioral rhythms become the foundation for our dance through life.

Rhythm is indeed an integral element in music. However, when the average nonmusician thinks about a song by their favorite artist, it is the melody that is remembered. What is the process for selecting the order and sequence of pitches that will produce a memorable melody? Is the process random or arbitrary? I think it will be helpful for us to pause here and spend a little time discussing the theory behind the music we listen to. The time that we will spend discussing these technical aspects of music will help you to better understand the source of not only melody but harmony too.

The A-B-C's of It

The vast majority of music made in Western culture is based on the seven notes contained in the following scale: A-B-C-D-E-F-G. There is a space of one whole step, or one whole tone that exists between most of the seven notes. However, there are two exceptions in our scale, one between B and C, and the other between E and F. In each of the exceptions, the space between the notes is one half step. There are other half steps between the notes, and they are called *sharps* and designated in musical notation by the symbol #. There are also *flats*, and they are designated in musical notation by the symbol ♭. A note that is one half step above a fundamental note is called a sharp (e.g., A and A-sharp). When a note is one half step below a fundamental tone, it is called a flat (e.g., B and B-flat). The raised note and the lowered note can be the same actual note on a piano, however they would be named differently depending on what key the musician is playing in. When those half tones are inserted into our scale it becomes what is called a chromatic scale. The notes in a chromatic scale beginning with A are as follows: A–A#–B–C–C#–D–D#–E–F–F#–G–G#. The majority of music we hear in the West is created with these twelve notes.

If I were reading the last paragraph without having had any musical training, I could find myself asking, why just twelve? Why is there not an A, an A-sharp, and then some other pitch before we land on the next whole tone, which is B? Actually it is possible to create additional pitches through manipulating an instrument or voice in such a way that other pitches become audible. Many non-Western cultures make music with these notes, but they are often not true tones, meaning that they do not occur naturally. How is this possible? By accessing something called the *overtone series*. It is from the overtone series that rules for our scales originate, and it is from the overtone series that our concept of harmony is formed.

I will now attempt to give you a very basic understanding of the overtone series. Let us begin by dissecting the word itself: *over* (that is, "above") and *tone* (that is, "sound"). If we were to reverse the order of the parts of this compound word, we would get "tone-over." This means that there are additional notes present above the note being played. These tones are present every time a note is struck, but they are inaudible to the human ear. For example, if the fundamental or dominant note is A, vibrating at 440 Hz, then the overtone series would consist of the note A = 440 Hz, followed by 880 Hz, then 1320 Hz, 1760 Hz and so on. Notice that the series of frequencies follows a set pattern of multiples beginning with the doubling of the value of fundamental tone. The interesting thing about the overtone series is that when a person sings or plays a single note, they are actually playing the aggregate of a series of notes. Typically only the bottom, or fundamental, pitch of the overtone series is distinguishable to the ear. Musicians can often manipulate their instruments to force the hidden tones that exist above the fundamental tone to be heard, and these sounds are called harmonics. Please take notice that the term *harmonic* is a relative of the word *harmony*. This will become important to our discussion at a later time.

Let us now look at some ways that the overtone series affects the melodies that we all love. In the last paragraph, we discussed the fact that tones are spaced in a symmetrical relationship to one another. This fixed spatial relationship between notes may influence which sequences of notes sound pleasing to the Western ear. Western scales and chord structures are created in such a way as not to violate the order in which the notes occur in the overtone series. These patterns become embedded in our psyche, and this causes us to prefer the sound of certain melodic patterns more than others. We become so accustomed to music being written in this fashion that when we hear music from other cultures that is not based on Western scales, we take it as unpleasant, strange, or substandard.

The Beautiful Root

Like the overtone series, a scale contains a fundamental note, or what musicians call the *root*. The root note becomes the baseline for the way that other notes relate to each other. The two scales most often used in the West are called the major scale and the minor scale. Here is a major scale with the note A as the root or fundamental tone: A–B–C#–D–E–F#–G#, and then A once more. The second A in the series is referred to as the octave. An octave is a note that is in reality the same note, but will sound several pitches higher or lower. Most of us have at one time or another looked at a piano keyboard. In fact when I was growing up, most kids that I knew could play "Chopsticks" on a piano. In order to play this song, kids would move their fingers up and down the keyboard simultaneously in a widening pattern. If you have ever played "Chopsticks," you know that if you move your fingers far enough apart from any one note on a piano, you will eventually run into that same note again. That note would be the octave. Why? A piano keyboard has seven whites keys and five black keys and then it repeats. If you were to strike the white key just to the left of the two black keys on a piano, then that would be the note C. If you then move your fingers in either direction, you will eventually run into another white key that is positioned just to the left of two black keys. You have just landed on the octave of your original note, C. The same would hold true for any other white key that you choose to strike first.

The Branches

Melody is created through sequencing notes in such a manner that they will sound pleasing to the ear, or express the idea or mood of the artist. There is an additional element in music that the overtone series influences, and that is harmony. Harmony blends the notes of a melody with other compatible notes. This can give the melody more power and greater texture. Harmony is also used to create something called a *chord*. A chord supports the melody and brings coherence to the music. Let us look at our A-major scale once more. This time I will not be speaking in terms of the frequency value of a note (e.g., A=440 Hz). Rather, I will be talking about the harmonic, or spatial, relationships between each note in the scale.

As we discuss harmony, it will be helpful to remember that I contend that melody is about the pitch and sound of notes. Harmony, on the other hand, is more about the space or distance between the notes of a particular scale. The distance between each note is called an *interval*. Intervals create both melody and harmony. The fact that I am drawing a distinction between how intervals affect music is simply a matter of preference on my part. We could easily reverse the emphasis, and what I have said about melody and harmony would still be true. Pitch, intervals, and scales are all necessary ingredients in music. Moving forward, we must remember that it is how these ingredients relate to each other that results in musical magic.

Let us now look at what constitutes an interval, and then we will discuss what that means. If we return once more to the A-major scale, and then add the interval designation to identify the space between each note, the sequence would look like this: A = Root or 1st, B = 2nd, C = 3rd, D = 4th, E = 5th, F# = 6th, G# = 7th, A = Octave. Please take notice of the number to the right of each note. That number designates its harmonic relationship to the root note of the scale. The root would be the *first*, the next note is the *second* (the second note closest to the root), and then the *third*, and so on. These numbers will have relevance as we discuss harmony. This might be a good time to consider that harmonic relationships can be illustrative of relationships between people too.

The *harmonic series*, of which the overtone series is a part, is where we get the template for what is good or bad harmony. Numerically the intervals of the harmonic series run as follows: root, octave, perfect fifth, perfect fourth, major third, minor third, subminor third, super major second, and the like. There are several other notes in the harmonic sound spectrum, but we will stop here because it only becomes more technical.

We have all heard music featuring multiple voices singing together around a melody. Even though all the voices were singing the same basic melody at the same time, the pitches that they were singing were very different from each other. They were different pitches, or notes, yet they seemed to blend seamlessly, creating a beautiful, almost ethereal, sound. That is harmony! Harmony is that special relationship between notes that allows them to complement, enhance, support, and bring out the best in the other. Harmony is a togetherness that results in the plural being stronger than the singular, in the sum being stronger than the parts. In sports, harmony is called teamwork. In the formation of insular social groupings, harmony is considered desirable because it serves as a bonding agent between the people. Even when it results in groupings that are completely homogenous in makeup, we view it as a positive. We call that form of harmonious positioning a demographic. We tailor our efforts at selling something to appeal specifically to certain demographics. In other words, harmonious relationships become a useful tool, but in race relations harmony is viewed differently. It is undervalued, and it is believed to be abnormal for people of one race to live in harmony with, or side by side, people of other races. A common assumption is that social harmony is impossible to achieve and therefore not worth pursuing. Why is this assumption so common?

Connecting the Branches

To this point I have attempted to familiarize you with the concept of harmony in the melodic sense. However, there is another way that musicians in the West use harmony that is relevant to our discussion, and that is the utilization of harmony to form chords. A chord is an arrangement of notes that can contain a melodic component, a rhythmic component, and a harmonic component. Chords contain all the musical elements previously discussed in this chapter, and they are the foundation on which songs are built. I believe that studying chords is a great way to open the conversation about what music can teach us about better race relationships.

Chords are the sounds that you hear when a singer uses a guitar or a piano as a lone accompanying instrument. Most of us have had the pleasure of watching a singer-songwriter as they sing their poetic verses over a strumming guitar. On a business trip or a vacation, perhaps you have found yourself in a hotel lounge that has a piano bar. The artist at the piano is singing a song while her hands rhythmically establish a cadence or beat on the keyboard. In both instances the musicians are using chords to *comp*. *Comp* is an interesting term because in many ways it could be taken as a sort of musician's double entendre. What if the word *comp* was actually an abbreviated form of one or both of these two words: *accompany* and *complement*? Let us first look at the word *accompany*. If the definition of *accompany* is "to do something with someone at the same time," then chords in fact do often accompany melodies. If we define the word *complement* as the action taken to complete something, then chords could be said to complete, and even to support and affirm the melody.

This is a good time to pause and to highlight correlations between the process of creating a chord harmonically and creating harmony in race relations. A musician typically spends a considerable amount of time thinking through which notes to use when forming the chords in a piece of music.

The eventual selection is arrived at because a great deal of consideration is given to the way the notes will relate to each other. Remember when we discussed scales a few pages ago? I said that the fundamental note dictates the way that other notes in a melody relate to one another. The same holds true with chords, and the same holds true for race relations. If the fundamental note, and by analogy the majority culture, is out of tune or poorly positioned, the relationship among the remaining notes (or people groups) will be negatively affected.

Blending the Branches

Orchestrating a song involves movements of notes that form melodies that are then supported by the chords we have been discussing. Chords and melodies are both based on the same fundamental note concept. When a fundamental chord moves on to another position on an instrument, that movement is called a *progression*. A blues song most often utilizes a one-four-five progression of chords. The musician would play the root chord for a set number of bars. The performer would then play the four chord for an additional number of bars, and then the five chord. If our blues song were in the key of C, then the root would be C. The four (IV) chord would be F, and the five (V) chord would be G. Counting four scale tones up from the root, or C, derives the numerical designation *four chord*. The *five chord* would then be positioned five scale tones up from the root. The one-four-five (I–IV–V) chord designation is of interest because the vast majority of songs in the American pop, country, rock, and blues genres are based on those three chords.

Musicians use chords to set moods. If a single note within a chord is changed, that change can make a huge difference. One example of this can be seen in something that occurred in our TOP program that I referenced earlier. We use a reggae song by Bob Marley titled "One Love." We do this to get the kids singing and thinking about the value of camaraderie. For those of you who are not familiar with this piece of music, it is an upbeat song calling for unity among all people. The chorus ends with the kids singing, "Let's get together and feel all right."

Our TOP program is mainly for youth between eight and twelve years old. We play that song and then ask them to sing along with us. Usually they are more than willing to join in because it is both a happy song and fun to sing. Here is an interesting thing that occurs during TOP. There have been times when we have lowered the third note in the chord, which changes the chord from a major chord to a minor chord. This one slight alteration made the kids not want to sing the song any longer. When asked why they stopped singing, they said, "Because the new sound made them sad rather than happy."

Composers use the chords that have proven to evoke pleasant, even joyous, audience responses over and over again. Musicians become reluctant to use chords that will not elicit a positive reaction from their audience. That is one reason that there is a lot of repetition in music. Our attempts to improve race relations often fall victim to the same scenario. We often look to the failed solutions from the past because "the audience" is at least comfortable with the sound of them. We seem hesitant to break free and alter the accepted way of doing things, even slightly. Change does not seem to happen when human beings are comfortable. Many scientists believe that openness to change comes through a process called disequilibrium. The basic idea behind that theory is when people are uncomfortable, they will welcome the opportunity to do things differently. The problem for the musicians who see the future is that it takes a lot of patience to wait for people to become uncomfortable listening to the old sound. Thankfully, in both race relations and music there always seem to be a few people who are not content to wait, who believe that the future is now.

Spontaneous Expression

A person who is courageous enough to function outside an accepted norm is usually rewarded with censure and quite often ostracism. They are called names such as troublemaker, maverick, or maybe even subversive. On many occasions they are even called arrogant, difficult, or in the community of faith, heretics. I grew up listening to the jazz musicians who pioneered the style referred to as hard bop and free jazz. You may or may not be that familiar with these particular styles of music because they were never able to achieve mainstream status. In my circle of friends these new forms were a welcome sound to our ears, in spite of their being quite revolutionary and controversial. People such as saxophonist Ornette Coleman, pianist Thelonius Monk, bassist Charlie Mingus, and my favorite musician, saxophonist John Coltrane, were called many of the names just listed above. Why? Because they simply wanted to alter the way melodies and chords were positioned. Their reward for attempting to improve the genre of jazz through innovation was that music critics accused them of trying to *ruin* the art form.

Ornette Coleman in particular had a very hard time getting his vision to gain acceptance and approval among the establishment. A famous trumpet player of his era named Miles Davis was said to have called him "psychotic." He said that because Mr. Coleman dared to use the same twelve notes that Miles himself was using, only in a different way. I remember a rumor circulating around that said another very big name in jazz showed up at Ornette's New York apartment at four in the morning wanting to "kick his butt." Why? In this instance it was because Ornette had the temerity to say that the traditional placement of chords in jazz needed to be changed in order to allow for more freedom. Why would the thought of another musician gaining the same amount of freedom that you enjoy be so upsetting? A follow-up question could be, why would the thought of marginalized people groups gaining the same amount of freedom and privilege as the majority group enjoys be so upsetting to some?"

In his era John Coltrane was considered heretical for altering harmonies, and stretching accepted tonal colorations. Ornette Coleman was chastised for eliminating dependence on chords as the foundational element for his playing. Bob Dylan was ridiculed for tweaking the traditional concept of vocal melody, and then worse, using electric guitars in American folk music. The willingness of these artists to venture into the realm of the unconventional earned each of them nothing short of scathing reviews from their peers, only to be followed by acceptance. Allow me to point out here that Ornette Coleman is still waiting for his long-overdue critical and commercial acceptance. Music is forever expanding, and that is a good and necessary process for its survival. When the new is folded into the old, it creates diversity. The more diversity that is created, the better the chances are for music's upward evolution. That is probably true for cultural diversity as well.

Diversity is an intimidating word to people whose brains have a default mechanism that says, "I prefer life like it has always been." In their minds the status quo suggests a form of stability. But how much stability ever really exists anyway? Today technology has brought people closer together than ever before. People groups that you once viewed as strange because distance had made their cultural habits unfamiliar to you are suddenly your neighbors. The geographical boundaries that once defined ethnic groups have been irreversibly altered because of globalization. Within a matter of hours a person who had once lived in Johannesburg, South Africa, can be signing a rental agreement for a new residence in Los Angeles, California.

There was a time when personal identity was determined by geographical roots more than by any cultural or personal identification. For example, if you were a Jamaican living in the U.S. then people would assume that you were like all other Jamaicans. It would not matter to them if you came from Kingston, a major city, or from a village in the mountains: you would still be simply Jamaican. Today's reality is that self-identity may actually trump a person's country of origin. This could be a hard pill to swallow for those who fear the prospect of diversity.

As I write this, a worldwide recession is in full swing in many parts of the Western world. The mood of the citizenry in these countries is one of pessimism and fear. Groups of people, like groups of notes, can express collective moods. The worldview of a racial group affects the overall mood of that group, just as the structure of the chord affected the mood of the kids during TOP. There are racial groups who, in a general sense, are happy with how their life's chord is structured. They are optimistic about who they are, and what life has to offer them. However there are other groups of people whose position in the societal "chord structure" more closely resembles a minor chord than a major chord. If you remember my TOP illustration, the minor chord elicited a sad reaction from the kids. Keep in mind that it took the repositioning of a single note to completely change the children's perception of Bob Marley's song from one of happiness to one of sadness. One slight change in the position of a note changed everything! It is the positioning of notes (and people groups) that decides whether harmony or discord is produced. Perhaps slight changes in the positioning of notes in the form of people groups could change everything too, only in a positive way.

5

Deliberate Diversity

In the year 1931 English writer Aldous Huxley penned a classic book titled *A Brave New World*. The novel was extremely popular in its day and to a degree prophetic. The story line depicted a society built around cultural hierarchies, including "savages" who lived in America. The book illustrates the tensions that can exist between a society of elites and the various subcultures that labor along beneath it. If we were to alter one word in this famous title, it would pretty much describe the times in which we live. How is this for a slogan for our time, *A Diverse New World*! It is hard to imagine that people living in Europe at the end of the last century could have envisioned Euro Zones for commerce, a common currency named the Euro, or an ethnographic map made up of so many darker-skinned peoples within the city limits of its major cities. Multiculturalism has come to most of Europe, and not everyone is excited about what that means. Diversification brings change, and for many that change is often accompanied by a plethora of emotions, ranging from uneasiness to high levels of fear.

The changes occurring on the European ethnographic map have had an effect on us who live in the United States as well. American society is structured and stratified based on the assumption that skin color is an indicator of separate biological categories. People that hold this view believe that the integration of these differently hued people will result in diluting what had existed before, and they find that rather disturbing. My experience in music assures me that this fear is unwarranted, but it appears to be gaining momentum even in today's "postracial" era. Perhaps we should put the brakes on, take a deep breath, and ask ourselves the following question: did music lose its purity and value when Coltrane, Dylan, and others crossed categorical borders? Absolutely not! In fact those very changes have resulted in more varieties of music being listened to and enjoyed by more people than ever. This happened because diversification had created new and different types of musical categories. To illustrate this, let us briefly turn to a genre that was once considered pretty traditioncentric: country music. Today you can listen to country pop, progressive country, country rock, Texas-styled country, and even something called cowpunk. The subcategories just listed are but a few of the styles that exist within the genre of country music today.

In the jazz genre there are categories for smooth jazz, hard bop, Latin jazz, jazz-fusion, swing, and several other forms. All of them are viewed as jazz music. The diversification process in music did cause some to experience a form of mild anxiety due to the uncertainty as to what direction the music was heading. As with many things in life people seem to be most comfortable when they have stationary categorical boxes to house their preferences. Categorical lines do become blurred during the process of diversification, but the results have proven to be worth the discomfort that diversification brings. Here is an example. I recorded several records with two friends named Clifford Coulter and Mel Brown. They were released on the Impulse label, and that was a leading jazz imprint at the time. For several years our music languished in obscurity until the emergence of Internet radio and YouTube. The creation of a wider variety of musical categories via these sources has kindled a rebirth of interest in the music that we had recorded.

The broadening of categories within music has resulted in more professional opportunity for musicians rather than less. The music we recorded decades ago now appeals to a younger and wider audience, including people that previously had no label to use to describe it. Some referred to the music as acid jazz, others thought that it was another form of the blues. Still others patted their feet to it thinking that it was funk. Labels aside, the music became attractive to a variety of demographic groups because diversity freed our music from any categorical restraints. Are there principles that can be carried over from the music arena to the social arena that could help remove social restraints by category? Sure there are. Perhaps letting go of the perception that allowing access to new "styles" of people would result in fewer opportunities for the majority would be a good start. Part of the anxiety that multiculturalism arouses in people is the fear that it will ultimately end with too much competition for too few resources. The thinking is that it will result in "our" group being left out. Our music was left out when the categories were narrow but found a home once categories were expanded through the diversification of delivery systems. Perhaps our example proves the being-left-out idea when diversity occurs is questionable at best.

Elitism on the Radio

Forty years ago local AM radio stations were the primary sources for popular music. *AM* stands for *amplitude modulation*. The call letters of an AM radio station, such as 540 AM, identify the frequency band that the music is broadcast over. The radio stations of that era typically specialized in a singular type of broadcasting format, meaning that only one musical style or genre was played. People rarely heard more than one genre of music being played per station. Even the style of music selected within the genre was narrowly focused. Listeners tuned their radio dial to the station they liked, and then listened to the music that they assumed they should like. Radio programmers controlled the playlists and occasionally restricted the playlists to their own preferences. When that occurred, listeners learned to like whatever it was the station offered. Station managers knew that many listeners would respond positively to whatever music was presented to them as long as it was played often enough. At that time Americans had just defeated the Axis powers—Germany, Japan and Italy—in a world war. Americans believed themselves to be the best. Since we believed that we were the best we had the best tastes, and so whatever style of music our radio stations offer us must be the best. It was quite reasonable for the listener to assume that the music they were hearing had to be the best. Even if a listener did not care for the music they were hearing, they would make the effort to develop a taste for the music, similar to the way a person can intentionally develop a taste for a new food product over time.

That is fine, but the result of homogenous radio programming was that the listener's musical palate became very bland and predictable. Listeners selected a radio station by genre loyalty. If a person liked rock and roll, they would tune their dial to the hypothetical rock station KJIM. If a person preferred country music, then KCAL would be the proper choice. Radio stations drew up Top Forty playlists, which included the forty most popular songs in a given musical genre or subgenre. The disc jockey (as the person who played the records was called) was often limited to the forty songs that were the most popular around the country. Disc jockeys would play those records regardless of the radio station's geographical location and regardless of dissimilarities in the tastes of their audiences, because those songs were purported to be national hits. However, as the 1960s were winding down, the complexity of the musical stylistic landscape was rapidly changing. Musicians were creating new styles within preexisting musical genres. Those new styles were disparate in sound and yet they were coterminous with previous musical boundaries. This means that the new forms of music were able to find a way to fit in with what was already there.

Think back to the time in our history when new states were being added to the United States of America. They were recently formed entities operating within our preexisting territorial boundaries, yet their formation did not have a negative effect on what had existed previously. When the dust settled, those new territories were coterminous, or able to share the same space with the existing states. *Coterminous* is a useful word for illustrating the process that artists used to fit in to the narrow parameters that radio stations had established. Artists adapted out of necessity because the only way they could have their music reach a wide audience was to give the decision makers at the stations exactly what they wanted. Unfortunately for them, what the radio people wanted was sameness. Most of the artists of that era were pressured into becoming cookie-cutter versions of each other. A similar pressure towards sameness and homogeneity exists in many of our cultural attitudes. People exert pressure, often unknowingly, on other people to accept the attitudes of their peers. This type of peer pressure ends up affecting the attitudes that people have about race. This eventually results in an artificial predisposition to prefer what is similar. The almost obsessive practice of preferring the same is what I call *similarism*.

Similarism is like a marketing concept that capitalizes on what many would believe to be the natural preference for what is similar and therefore familiar. The assumption that we prefer folks similar to ourselves is based on the belief that a mechanism inside every person alerts the brain whenever the person comes into contact with something or someone like them. Thinkers from Plato to French philosopher René Girard have put forward the concept of a mimetic impulse resident in each of us. The mimetic impulse stems for the word *meme*, which is defined as "an idea, behavior, or style that spreads from person to person within a culture."[1] The majority of people in our culture have called this inclination towards imitating each other peer pressure. The theory of the mimetic impulse and the popular notion of peer pressure both articulate the same idea that my term similarism does. The basic concept is this, likes follow likes—likes prefer likes. But is this inclination toward similarism a by-product of nature or nurture? Our media, both print and visual, have certainly had a hand in making this phenomenon so prevalent. Watch a television commercial. Notice that when couples are interacting in a situation, they are most often of the same race. This perpetuates the notion that it is natural to prefer, and then only associate with people who are visually like you. Let us turn back the clock a bit to look at the most recent time period when AM radio was still king in America.

Unique Sameness

Elvis Presley was the prototypical rock star with his perfectly coiffed hair and hip wiggle. His ascent to the top of AM-radio playlists spawned dozens of clones. Many of them become successful. Later the Beatles appeared on a popular American television show sporting what was affectionately called "mop top" haircuts. The Beatles influence permeated every area of pop culture. The only accurate way to describe the onslaught was to call it an "invasion." Not only did other musicians get Beatle haircuts, the average school kid did as well. The Beatle era marked the beginning of the merchandizing of musical art and musical artists. You could buy over one hundred Beatle items not related to their music. Up for sale were Beatle dolls, Beatle beds, Beatle cookies, and even Beatle perfume. If you were entrepreneurial during that era, and you placed the word Beatle before whatever product you had, it would more than likely sell. Full disclosure here: I was caught up in the wave of Beatlemania just as my friends were. I actually toyed with the idea of sporting a Beatle wig for a short period of time—a blond one at that!

You may be wondering why an African American kid with naturally curly hair would subject himself to wearing an unnatural-looking wig in order to have straight locks. The simple answer is that I wanted to follow the fad of the day. I thought I would absolutely die if I could not be like everybody else. At that time, mine was a similaristic thought pattern. This

---

1. *Wikipdia*, s.v., "Meme," line 1

phenomenon is very much like what happens when a person is caught up in the latest trend in any area of life, whether food, clothing, music, or what have you. There seems to be a subtle type of internal pressure that leads people to conform to whatever is "in" at any given time.

Similarism operates on the assumption that most things in life can be assigned a category, and those categories not only describe; they define. Once a person's individual category is identified, a kind of expectation enters the psyche, which encourages one to behave in a similar manner to everyone else within that category. If you are a rocker, then bring on the body piercings and tattoos. If you are a European American, then you must develop a speech pattern consistent with the rest of that group. If you are a Hispanic person, then you are obligated to develop a way of dressing and walking that is different from the way that the blacks dress and walk, who live just a few blocks away.

Anthropologists and sociologists have formed many of their opinions about race by studying the similarities they find in the daily habits of people living in a particular geography. Then these scholars convert their opinions into data that shape their views concerning what an entire people group was or is like. Book after book has been published informing readers what it means to be human within specific groups. Such investigation soon gave way to the idea that distinct races actually exist and can be identified by skin color, place of birth, music preference, diet—even from something as transient as wardrobe selection. The process was to observe, classify, and then place human beings into their distinct categorical type.

Like social scientists, professionals within the music industry had at one time created rigid categories for musical styles. Some of those categories were based on the types of instruments used, or on the number of voices utilized to sing it, even down to the music's cadence and volume. I have a vivid recollection of a time when I asked a jazz-musician friend who had attended a rock concert what style of music the band had played. He answered, "Loud!" The establishment of one categorical type automatically opens the door for the possibility of categorical error. It should be considered a mistake to suggest that *loud* is a musical category. *Loud* is not necessarily a style or category unto itself because every type of music can be performed loudly.

Darker-skinned people cannot be a true category unto itself either. Just think: most of what people with darker skin do each day is also done by the people with lighter skin, so why is there the need for a separate category? All forms of music can be performed loudly, and people of every skin hue can excel at sports, music, dance, or whatever else, and yet stereotypes linger on, often leading to categorical error. I realize what I am about to say will be somewhat difficult for people born after 1980 to conceptualize, but this was both sad and true. There was a time when the dividing lines between musical categories was so rigid that people even drew a distinction between a white or black musician performing the identical song. Allow me to take you back in time for a moment.

Divisions by Race

In 1957 rock-and-roll pioneer Fats Domino sang a song titled "I'm Walking." When he performed the song, it was considered to be "black music." A short while later a white teen idol named Rick Nelson sang the very same song, following the same basic arrangement, and somehow the song magically became "white music"—simply because a white male performed it. It is true that this happened quite a few decades ago. It is also true that much of the thinking that led to this situation has gone by the wayside. Sadly, that scenario continues to occur all too frequently in postracial America. I do acknowledge that progress has been made, but we still have quite a distance to go before we let go of color codes for making decisions. Far too many people still hold on to the notion that music has a racial component to it. Many people out there make their decision about which musical style they prefer based on the skin color of the performer. For example, for several years the person with the most sales in what is considered to be a black genre, hip-hop, was a white performer named Eminem. In spite of Eminem's success in the genre most white people still perceive hip-hop to be black folks' music and avoid it. There is no question in my mind that music is much further along the diversification path than the greater society—but old habits do seem to hang on way past their usefulness—even when it comes to tastes in music.

Several shifts within the music business coalesced in the 1960s and '70s and led to the music business becoming more diversified. One shift affected how radio was done. A different delivery system for music to travel the airwaves called FM (frequency-modulation) radio supplanted AM radio as the most popular broadcast medium. When FM became so enormously popular it broke the artificial boundaries that the Top Forty AM stations had established during the preceding decades. FM-radio listeners were now able hear a song by folk singer Bob Dylan, followed by Jimi Hendrix playing rock. A listener could hear a song by a country artist such as Glenn Campbell segueing into a song by a rhythm-and-blues vocal group on the Motown label. These diverse styles were played during the same radio program, and that changed everything. Remember that the older AM format was narrowly focused on one style of music, and the DJs were rarely allowed to play any variety. This new access to musical variety encouraged listeners to go out and purchase products from multiple sources. The music business had just expanded its market share because of the many music purchases that occurred across demographic boundaries. Given the rise of FM and the expanding music business from the mid-1960s to the mid-1970s, this span is considered the golden age of rock.

Boxes

Musical diversity had finally come to America's listening habits. With that came a more pluralistic understanding about the very essence of music. Today with the extensive amount of digitized music available, many people listen to anything they choose without giving it a second thought. The iPod and other portable digital music-delivery systems can hold literally thousands of songs. This has resulted in songs by diverse artists no longer being restricted to the categorical boxes that their music was originally placed in. The truth is those boxes were often created by "suits"—lawyers and record executives who were not musicians. In fact, those once-rigid categorical boxes have now been rendered irrelevant by heightened consumer sophistication.

For centuries the majority of human beings rarely traveled more than a few miles from their place of birth. Just as the musical styles of the 1950s were separated into categorical boxes, so in most previous centuries people were expected to remain in their own geographical "boxes," and they did. All of that has changed as a result of the access to transportation that most enjoy today. Perceptions of where one belongs have been radically modified through what we call globalization. The term *globalization* means different things to different people. Economic experts, anthropologists, political leaders, and sociologists all use the term, but they apply it in different ways, and for dissimilar reasons. Regardless of who uses the term, or why, it always suggests that some type of boundary has been crossed. This means that the perceived distance between people has become shorter. To many the term *globalization* signals an end to the "our way" ethos that for centuries has caused people to intentionally distance themselves from each other. Those who fear globalization believe that the process of crossing boundaries will result in a borderless society, and that prospect is very unsettling. They find the prospect of diversification more than a little disturbing.

When musical diversity came to America, it was a very important event. Concert halls and other venues became more integrated when a diverse fan base followed their favorite artist. Suddenly musicians were willing to risk too. They risked everything so that new forms of music could be heard. They put their livelihoods in jeopardy to break away from the stodgy, monotonous routine that other musicians had to endure due to unrelenting commercial pressure. A term that many used to identify these musical pioneers in the genre of jazz was *avant garde*. Many believe that term to be a cognate of two words that describe the military units that would scout the enemy's position before a battle. They were called the "advance guards." We all know that the future will arrive at some point in time. Fear of what that will look like can prevent some from truly desiring its arrival. Musicians must imagine the future in order to prepare for it, or be left behind. My experience in the music business taught me the importance of preparation, and the same may hold true for people in every walk of life. Becoming deliberate about diversification begins with preparation too. A prepared mind can be an open mind, with a little effort.

Life Outside the Box

My wife, Julaine, and I have a few close friends; among them are Robert and Kimberly. They are professional people, and they each hold multiple graduate degrees. They are in their early forties, and both of them are of European descent. Their son, Ian, is nine years old at this writing, and he has already been exposed to a multicultural way of life. One of his recent birthday parties resembled the United Nations because of the different ethnicities of the children invited. Ian's parents are also preparing him for a time when English may not necessarily be the lingua franca of his environment. They are purposely raising Ian to be multilingual by exposing him to both Spanish and French. They understand that a time may soon arrive when national boundaries will have become so relaxed that being multilingual will be not simply a good idea; it will be an essential. I have been present when Ian has abandoned his very proper English speech pattern in order to break out singing in Spanish. Then at lunch this past week, Ian was playfully speaking to me in French.

Another example of outside-the-box thinking is the way that our good friends José and Evette are educating their children. Their children speak English at school and Spanish at home while studying a Chinese dialect privately. Evette and Jose's children are friends with Ian as well. Now here is where it gets good: All the children just mentioned are friends with some other children who are equally interesting. Their father is named François, and he is a Jamaican American. Their mother is named Anh, and she is a Vietnamese American who is fluent in Spanish. These children are well on their way to being prepared for life in a pluralistic society. Are you?

Robert and Kimberly, Ian's parents, have a hopeful attitude about the future of race relations. They not only involve themselves in activities that advance better race relations; they are instilling a hopeful attitude in their son. Nurturing a child is similar to creating music. Both are artistic endeavors that require a great deal of preparation and flexibility. I believe that when Ian is older, his ability to speak multiple languages will have prepared him to appreciate people from cultures other than his own. Additionally, I believe he will be prepared to view those people as his equals in the truest sense of the word. Would it not be wonderful if Ian's generation was the first to enter adulthood not assuming that it is natural to socialize along the lines drawn by skin color?

Like most kids today, Ian is being taught that everyone is equal. The important thing is that his parents are instilling in him the idea that he has an almost sacred responsibility to treat everyone equally. There really is a difference between belief and responsibility, and one does not always follow the other. Beliefs without action accomplishes very little. Many believe in the concept of equality, but acting on those stated beliefs about race happens very infrequently. Hopefully the kids just mentioned will do a better job of putting action behind their professed attitudes about race when they are older.

Just as, when it comes to race relations, sameness and similarism are easy to uphold, so even within an enterprise as progressive as music, unfortunately, there seems to be a tendency for some musicians to default to sameness. The reason for this could be that many musicians develop their skill through mimicking other musicians. This then leads those musicians to play the same music in the same way over and over again until it reaches a state of unbearable monotony. If we continue relating to other human beings the same way that we always have, it will produce an unbearable state of monotony within our society as well. In the paragraphs that follow, we will briefly look at a musical genre that had a reputation for giving its musicians the freedom to explore new ways of expression through improvisation: jazz. But in order to discuss one way that jazz broke away from the cycle of monotony, I introduce two new terms—one is *polyphonic*, and the other is *polytonal.*

Beauty in the Multiple

Several years ago a reading program called *Hooked on Phonics* became very popular. The program used sounds, together with the more traditional visual approach, to teach children to read. A phonic is simply a sound. Musically speaking, phonics are the overall sounds that musicians use to emote and express themselves. The word *polyphony* describes a situation where multiple melodic sounds or *phonics* occur simultaneously. The word *polytonal* describes a situation where multiple tones in the form of pitches and chords occur simultaneously. When jazz greats Ornette Coleman and John Coltrane began to speak in a new musical vocabulary on their instruments, they utilized both polyphonic and polytonal elements in their music. This caused many listeners and critics alike to be so alarmed that they asked, "Say what?" Appreciation for the new forms that they were experimenting with was not immediate; nor was it very widespread. However the end result of their visionary excursions into different tonal combinations produced an overall sound that had not yet existed. It also brought about the diversification within jazz that continues on to this day.

Two things were necessary for this new style of music, called free jazz, to be accepted as legitimate. First, Coleman and Coltrane had to explain to the critics what it was they were doing, and why they were doing it. Second, they had to wait patiently for the average jazz aficionado to develop an appreciation for their new style. Even professional musicians needed time to adjust in order to understand what it was Coleman and Coltrane were playing. It was a totally revolutionary concept to have multiple melodies coexisting in multiple keys and with multiple chords. Stop and think about that concept in a purely sociological context. If different races were analogous to polytones within a piece of music, then different races would be occupying the same space at the same time. And they would do so in complete harmonic peace with each other. If the preferences and outlooks of different racial groups were analogous to polyphony, then those preferences would not be characterized as competing or conflicting "melodies" but as complementary. In the genre of jazz these two concepts of polyphony and polytonality paved the way for a multiplicity of sounds being accepted as something normal and even beautiful in popular music. I sense the same will occur when people realize that there is beauty in the multiplicity of people types.

Diversity assumes that when cultures mix, new sounds will emerge. The new sounds that emanate out of this polytonal/polyphonic cultural mix will come in the form of new words, customs, foods, and values. I grew up in an urban setting, and I played music that was later called funk. The musical meaning of the word *funk* stems from musicians in the African American community referring to certain musical patterns as dirty, stinky, and even nasty sounding. Obviously these words would be viewed as negative if you were describing a person, but in musical vocabulary they were accepted as describing something good.

For example, if one were to like a particular song she or he might say, "That's funkier than a gorilla's armpit." That would be a compliment! Today the word *funk* is being used by many Anglo Americans but with a different meaning. Today that group uses the word *funky* to describe something that is cool, hip, even exciting—and not something nasty. Do you see how the word *funk* is now both polytonal and polyphonic in application? Allow me to illustrate from personal experience the need to develop an appreciation for our two *poly-* words. Appreciation for the new and different may not simply come to you. You might actually have to make room for it.

A Higher Appreciation

In college I was required to take a music-appreciation class, and my teacher's name was Darryl Johnston. He was also my music-theory professor, and he was an avid classical-music aficionado. I recall him standing before our class and proclaiming that the classical composer Johann Sebastian Bach was the greatest musician that had ever lived. I remember thinking at the time, that can't be true because John Coltrane is the best musician that has ever lived! I do not remember how many students were in the room that day. A safe estimate is probably twenty. If my guess is accurate, it should not be difficult to imagine that there were twenty additional opinions silently expressed inside that room that day. I remember thinking that my teacher was not only wrong about Bach, but also arrogant to assume that his musical tastes were superior to the tastes of the others in the room. Then I realized that my objection to his opinion was partly based on my own arrogance, as evidenced by my belief that my preferences were far superior to his. At the time I was involved with some of the finest jazz musicians in the San Francisco Bay Area. In my mind a jazz musician was by nature far superior to a rocker, a folk-music performer, and definitely a classical musician. My thinking was that since classical musicians had to read their music instead of improvising, they had to be inferior. In my young mind jazz musicians were the standard by which every other musician should be judged. Period!

Did that last sentiment sound familiar? It should, because that is the same way that race pride works. Folks from each race considers that their preferences are the absolute best, and it becomes difficult for them to see any value in the preferences of others. Fortunately, something happened to cause a change in my outlook. I began Mr. Johnson's class loving one kind of music and strongly disliking some other types. As a result of my required listening assignments, and through the listening process itself, I learned how to appreciate other forms of music. I learned to listen, and listen with my heart open enough to hear the beauty in something that I had previously disliked. We would sit and listen to some piece of music over and over again, and that would be our class for that day. It amazed me that I was getting college credit for listening to music. For a while I believed I was skating by because it seemed too easy. However as time elapsed, I came to understand how difficult it is to listen properly. Listening is not just hearing something. It is listening with the genuine hope of understanding.

I once judged classical music unfairly in part because it was something that I would never take the time to create or perform. This means my personal preference clouded my ability to see the objective value of an entire genre of music. Establishing standards according to my own preferences proved not to be the best for me as a musician. My musical-appreciation class taught me to not judge the musical offering of another artist, and to respect the choices made by that artist.

It should go without saying that it is best not to judge the artistic offering of another, especially when that artist is God. Music-appreciation class also taught me that if I would listen to music with the ear of an open heart, instead of the ear of my own biases, it would be possible for me to enjoy a wide variety of music. In the Bible the heart is more than simply a body part. It often symbolizes the essence of what it means to be human. The heart can be said to be the place where a person's spirit, consciousness, and understanding reside. Music speaks to the heart through the ear. To reach a higher appreciation for people who we perceive to be different from us, we may just need to learn to listen—and listen not only to hear, but also to learn from them. Remember, learning from diverse streams of opinion is an acquired skill and a skill worth pursuing.

6

Ordering Diversity

Evolutionary change has a role in the way music and societies become ordered. This idea is simple enough, and most of us assume that the changes that have occurred within music over the years resulted from some type of upward evolution. However, music's actual progress may not result from evolution as much as from the fact that it is first created, arranged, cultivated, and then ordered by the artist. Remember that Western music is made up of only eleven notes. This means that music's advancement is actually achieved by the reordering of those eleven notes, and then by placing these arrangements of notes in different positions to achieve different results (different songs or symphonies). That reordering process would be called *diversification* in today's vernacular. Just as musical notes are ordered and arranged to create melodies, songs, and symphonies, people groups too were created, arranged, and then ordered into larger systems that we call culture. Music has progressed over the years because the musicians of the past were not opposed to reordering the notes to create a different and better sound.

In our society today there are many people who are put off at the very sound of the word *diversity*. But music has proved diversity to be a positive and necessary tool for its advancement. The ordering of diversity in music resulted in classical music dividing into subsets with names such as Renaissance, Baroque, Rococo, and Modern, among others—and they were all accepted as genuine classical music. It is possible that music lovers living in the Western world at that time were not even aware of the stylistic changes as they happened. The changes were many, the styles very diverse, but the music was performed in such a way that a thread of similarity tied the stylistic changes together, creating a united whole. Diversity is built into the way music is ordered, and it is my contention that diversity is built into the entire universe—including the way racial groups should be ordered.

Many musicologists believe the *classical era* refers to one specific time period within Western music. They would draw a distinction between musical periods: *baroque* music was composed in the seventeenth century, and the music of the eighteenth century is called *classical*. Such musicologists would then assign separate names (*baroque* and *classical*) for each of those music styles. I will be using the term *classical* to refer to the music that was popular in Europe from about the eleventh century continuing on through today. Today many people consider the music of this period to be stodgy and a bit boring when comparing it with popular music. This might simply be because there were no electric guitars, synthesizers, or digitized drum machines that would make the music interesting to modern tastes. The reality is that this music of the period was anything but tame. Actually it was quite revolutionary to the musicians and audiences of the day.

Classical music began its ascent to popularity during the time period called the High Middle Ages. Cultural shifts are not things that are date certain. There are a variety of opinions as to when the ancient era transitioned to the Middle Ages, and then to the modern era. My understanding is that the classical era as in Western music was loosely sandwiched between the "Middle Ages, approximately 400 to 1450,"[1] and the "Renaissance and Romantic periods."[2] Dating the stylistic transitions is difficult because many historians and observers of culture tend to date differently for different reasons. These time periods can be confusing because professionals working in the fields of art, music, science, and the humanities each use slightly different beginning and ending dates for each period. For our purposes it is only important to note that classical music had a popularity run of slightly over four hundred years.

Every cultural shift, including the one that occurred between the medieval and modern eras, brings with it a fresh understanding related to every aspect of life, including music. The medieval period had been basically premodern in the way it viewed the world. That worldview was almost

---

1. Britannica.com/, s.v. "Middle Ages," para. 1.

2. Naxos.com/, s.v., "History of Classical Music," sections 1,4.

the direct opposite of our modern worldview. Premodernity placed God at the center of human concern, and because of that, the people of that time viewed life pretty much through a spiritual lens. The modern worldview places scientific inquiry at the top of human concern, and spiritual matters are often relegated to the category of superstition. For instance, the majority of premodern people took for granted the existence of more than one realm of reality. They were quite comfortable acknowledging a visible and invisible cosmos. Questions like, who is God? and, what is God like? took center stage. For this reason the majority of the paintings from the period depicted religious themes. The type of music from that period was simple in composition, and it utilized singular melodies called *monotones*. While the music was very beautiful, it was really not all that interesting to some historians, due to its lack of complexity. A good example of that style would be the Gregorian chants sung in Roman Catholic churches.

During this time period a writer named Dante Alighieri penned a poem titled *The Divine Comedy* that depicts a dichotomous spirit/matter structure for explaining the cosmos—that is, how the universe is ordered. In the poem Dante puts forward a compelling argument that the cosmos is made up of different sets of hierarchies in the form of concentric spheres where God, the angels, and other heavenly beings reside. Within Dante's configuration there exists a sphere for the physical universe that is detached from the spiritual realm. Italian science writer Davide Castelvecchi describes Dante's system this way: "Dante's entire universe— both physical and spiritual—consists of two sets of concentric spheres, one centered at Earth, the other at God. If you were to point a laser vertically up toward the sky from any point on Earth, you'd be pointing it straight at that single point where Dante places God." [3]

If we were to slightly alter the definition of *cosmos* as the manner in which the universe was not only ordered but also structured, we would get a picture of the way Dante saw the world. Author George Eldon Ladd offered a definition of the word *cosmos* that may be helpful for you to see what it is I am putting forward. His definition is taken from the Greek word *kosmos*, and he says, "it is something which is in proper order or harmony, something which enjoys proper arrangement." [4] Combining Dante's hierarchical type of cosmic schema, and Ladd's harmonious definition helps describe the music of the medieval period. It cannot be emphasized strongly enough that the music of this period was very much about structure and ordered arrangements.

3. Castlevechi, "Dante's Universe, and Ours." http://www.pbs.org/wgbh/nova/blogs/physics/2012/07/dantes-universe/.

4. Ladd, *Gospel of the Kingdom*, 25

The transition from the medieval to the modern era introduced a different understanding about the way the world was ordered. Science replaced "the spiritual" as the filter through which life was analyzed. The human being became the subject matter that piqued the curiosity of philosophers, scientists, and artists, instead of God. It was also the time period when the idea of racial categories came into prominence. Scientists began to examine human traits and characteristics with the hope of unlocking the mystery of human variation. Science by definition cries out for certainty and order. At the time it seemed natural to "scientifically" create rigid human racial categories by skin color. The concept of genuine racial groupings was codified within the scientific community, and then embedded in the minds of the people outside the scientific community. With this codification a sense of order and manageability came into new fields of scientific, human-centered investigation. Within a short time the discipline of anthropology, or the study of what it means to be human, came into being.

Science was fast becoming the darling of the educated class. Science was also beginning to have a major impact on music. A German musician named Lorenz Christoph Mizler von Kolof created a society to explore music scientifically, "advocating the establishment of a musical science based firmly on mathematics and philosophy, and the imitation of nature in music."[5] Prior to this time, music had been transferred among musicians orally. However, now with the invention of the printing press, composers could preserve and potentially immortalize their music through the use of printed musical notation. Musicians could compose a score, record it on paper, and then have it performed exactly as the composer had intended. This new method of creating music resulted in individual expression and interpretation becoming less desirable. However, the upside was that this newly acquired method of creating music on paper eventually allowed for more complexity in the music. Composers now had the capability to sit in their writing space, and with strokes of a pen, layer elaborate musical parts on top of other parts. They were able to weave those parts into very complex musical scores. This complexity required multiple instruments to perform. Musical performance groups grew in size from small performing troupes into very large orchestras.

Composers began to write down their music at the same time that philosophers and scientists began to preserve and spread their speculations about race via the printing press. Perhaps because the printing-press

5. Bach-Cantatas.com/, s.v., "Lorenz Christoph Mizler von Kolof," section 3, line 1.

technology was fresh and exciting, people accepted these printed specula-tions about race as being absolute truth. One theory says that human beings do not learn from receiving short bursts of information, but learn through repeated telling of a story or concept. In other words, the more often a premise is put forward by a trusted source, in this instance printed reading materials, the more believable it becomes. Repetition is certainly one way that stereotype and cliché can move from myth status to accepted truth. A common axiom says whatever is repeated often enough can become a self-validating fact. Repetition is a very useful tool for creating music, however, when racial stereotype is what is being repeated it has a deleterious effect on race relations.

I have selected three classical composers to study because today they are considered masters, even geniuses, of their distinct musical styles. They were also transformative figures historically because much of the music that we listen to today is derived from concepts that they invented. There was a slight difference between the styles of music that each of them com-posed, and yet there was also a degree of commonality. The three compos-ers are Johann Sebastian Bach, Wolfgang Amadeus Mozart, and Ludwig von Beethoven. Let us begin with the person that a college professor of mine once called "the greatest musician that has ever lived": the famed Ger-man composer Johann Sebastian Bach.

Johann Sebastian Bach

Picture a time when music was understood to be more than simply an en-tertainment product. It may be difficult for us to imagine music as more than entertainment in the days of the iPod and of *American Idol*. At one time popular music was viewed as an integral part of a church service al-most on par with the reading of Scripture and the sermon. This was the environment in which Johann Sebastian Bach (1685–1750) composed his music. Bach was the consummate church musician, and he was a devoutly religious person. In fact, one article that I read said this about his music, "Nearly three fourths of Bach's 1,000 compositions were written for use in worship. All of his music was closely bound to Biblical text. At the end of much of his music Bach wrote: 'Soli Deo Gloria' (To God Alone be the Glory), or the initials SDG."[6] This illustrates perfectly that the music pro-duced by a musician is often a window into the very soul of that musician.

6. ReformationSA.org/, s.v., "Johann Sebastian Bach," para. 8

In fact, a musician's art often reflects the way that a particular musician perceives the world. In Bach's case, he was a musical theologian.

Bach was also a musical genius, but his genius did not prevent him from having to endure some struggles during his lifetime. One struggle had to do with his music. Apparently certain sounds that Bach wanted to incorporate into his music, his church deemed to be evil. Remember our conversation about intervals and spatial relationships? What the church was up in arms about was Bach's decision to flatten certain scale tones. They were so up in arms that "the Church Council resolved to reprimand Bach on his 'strange sounds' during the services."[7] But please do not become too judgmental about seventeenth-century values because of a belief that succeeding generations have evolved past them. In many of our churches today, some view the use of certain electronic instruments and certain chord patterns as inappropriate. Why? One reason could be that many Christian musicians and rock musicians use similar musical forms. Rock music is perceived to be evil, and so anything that sounds similar to rock must be evil too. If church leaders view rock to be evil, it is hard for them to see music as neutral. Their perspective is that music is either sacred or secular, and it cannot be both. The secular-vs.-sacred tension just mentioned was alive and well in Bach's time too.

Those who know the Bible can nevertheless overlook something recorded in the seventh chapter of the book of Mark. In one passage there, Jesus teaches the religious leaders of his day a valuable lesson related to perceptions. He cautions them that undesirable attitudes come from inside the human heart more so than from external influences (vv. 14–16). Today's accepted behavior pattern reflects an opposite understanding about moral and cultural contamination from what Jesus understood in Mark. We frequently prohibit ourselves from enjoying certain styles of music or from associating with people who live secular lifestyles. We might even avoid associating with people who have different cultural outlooks, due to our fear of being influenced away from "proper" Christian behavior. I was once told that the music I performed during my professional music years was directly responsible for people taking drugs and participating in wild sexual escapades. That may have been true about a few people, but it would certainly not have been true for everyone who attended our concerts.

False dichotomies tend to lead people in the direction of a very narrow either/or mentality. When musicians, and people of different cultures,

7. Baroquemusic.com/, s.v., "Arnstadt, 1703–1707," para. 4

are confronted with the new or different, they generally assume they have only two choices: to prefer their own or to prefer the new. The choice that seems to come most naturally is to prefer the familiar. Perhaps there are two takeaways concerning the treatment that Johann Sebastian Bach received that are worth noting. The first is that the appreciation of art is rarely permanent, and most art usually has an expiration date affixed to its popularity. The second takeaway comes from the adverse reaction exhibited towards Bach's new sound. People simply did not want to hear it. Sadly, the way people in the church reacted to Bach's music is similar to the way that many in the church today react to conversations about inclusion. They simply do not want to hear it.

Can we, or should we, close our ears to every style of music that is different from our own preferred style? Is it logical to make judgments about any one style of music when so much diversity exists within music? Should people in the church ostracize an individual, or even a group of people, because someone's musical palate is broader than their own? Bach was known to be an exemplary Christian. Yet the simple flattening of a few notes in his music caused some to be willing to diminish the substance of his character to such a degree that he came under severe attack. Time has proven that Bach's critics were wrong in their judgment concerning his commitment to the church. We now understand that he simply heard a sound, albeit different, and time has proven that sound to be just as good as what had preceded it. Perhaps it would be good to take a lesson from the life of Johann Sebastian Bach by no longer being critical of racial groups that "sound" different from your own.

Wolfgang Amadeus Mozart

Wolfgang Amadeus Mozart (1756–1791) is our second composer and he was very much influenced by our first example: Bach. John Solum writes: "It was in London that young Mozart met and befriended Bach's son Johann Christian Bach."[8] Author Robert W. Gutman writes, "Christian [was] one of the finest operatic talents of his time and [was] a significant influence on the young Mozart."[9] Bach's influence on Mozart was extensive and lasting: "Mozart's act of transcribing Bach's fugues, enabled Bach, who died earlier in the same decade in which Mozart was born, to become Mozart's

8. Hanover Ensemble, *Music for Lord Abingdon*, program notes.

9. Gutman, *Mozart: A Cultural Biography*, 148.

teacher—from his grave!"[10] Classical music evolved and advanced through the process of its practitioners' building on the work of their predecessors. They meticulously handed down technique, style, form, and harmonic structure to those who followed.

Just as composers passed on knowledge to their successors, our culture hands down many of its characteristics and attitudes to succeeding generations—often unintentionally. There are many cultural biases that we pass along from generation to generation that could be described as negative. United States history is replete with examples of not being all that welcoming to people who were different from the majority. At various times the inhospitable treatment once reserved for Native Americans and African peoples was expanded to include Jewish, Irish, Italian, Latino and Asian immigrants. Frankly, is it not true that we have a very long tradition of branding many different groups as "the other"? Typically the process of othering runs as follows: the majority culture embeds the perception of difference and inferiority into the cultural psyche through the use of negative stereotyping and myth. These myths are then handed down in much the same manner that music styles were handed down during the classical period.

Mozart is important to our discussion because his life could be viewed as a "type," or a prefiguring, of the obstacles and struggles that many minorities encounter throughout their lives. He was poor, he suffered ill health, and he was grossly misunderstood during his lifetime and that led to him being rejected quite frequently. In my opinion Mozart was also a futurist in many respects. At a time when most composers restricted their writing to one niche, Mozart was writing symphonies, operas, piano concertos, and music for smaller ensembles. He stretched preexisting boundaries so much that, as one writer says of him, "Mozart destroyed neoclassicism in opera. This was quite clearly understood by his contemporaries."[11] One of his contemporaries named Johann Wolfgang von Goethe wrote of Mozart's enormous impact on music in his *Italian Journal,* "All of our effort to confine ourselves to what is simple and limited was lost when Mozart appeared."[12]

Mozart's genius was not always well received or appreciated. Remember the aphorism "A rocker's lot is not always a happy one" from chapter 3? "Not a happy one" certainly describes Mozart's life as well. His music

10. Rasmussen, "Bach, Mozart, and the 'Musical Midwife,'" para. 40.

11. Rosen, *Classical Style,* 176.

12. *Wikipedia,* s.v., "Die Entführung aus dem Serail," section 5, para. 2.

did not gain widespread popularity until after his death, as evidenced by this quote from Harold C Shonberg's excellent book called *The Lives of the Great Composers*: "Thanks to the great success of *The Magic Flute*, there was a Mozart boom at his death."[13] I find it a bit ironic that a person who was in some respects a lightening rod, would someday have named for him a psychological treatment to calm patients, called the Mozart effect. The Mozart effect entails the idea that listening to Mozart's music makes people smarter, improves mental functions, and induces a sense of calm. Even if his music calms present-day listeners, Mozart's life disrupted the entire musical establishment of his time. As I mentioned earlier, *disequilibrium* is a word used in systems theory that suggests instability within a system is a necessary ingredient for change. Today when most people restrict their racial interaction to one niche, a little disruption to the "social infrastructure" might be called for. Perhaps the instability that would follow might produce an opening to usher in legitimate change moving forward. Mozart stretched the musical boundaries of his day and it is possible for us to stretch the racial boundaries that exist at this time.

Mozart's ability to straddle many stylistic fences while maintaining musical integrity is fascinating. Being that he was comfortable writing symphonies, it would have been easy, almost natural, for him to say, "I am a symphonic writer, and so why should I concern myself with opera." Similarly a person who is an educator could say, "Why should I concern myself with tennis?" I realize that what I've just said could seem a bit absurd on the surface, but this is pretty much the logic we use when we narrow our associations down to one specific group, or, "my people." Far too many folks in our society are comfortable saying, "I am happy living in my African American community, and so why should I concern myself with people in the white community?" Others are equally comfortable saying, "I am comfortable living in my all-white surroundings, and so why should I concern myself with what is going on with people with darker skin?" Had Mozart succumbed to the pressure to be limited to the familiar options in the musical style that he chose to pursue, all music would have suffered. When people succumb to any type of pressure that says, "Limit your human interaction to your own group," then all of humanity suffers.

Another interesting fact about Mozart relates to our discussion, and that has to do with his ethnic background. For quite some time there has been a running debate as to whether or not Mozart was Jewish. If you

13. Shonberg, *Lives of the Great Composers*, 108.

Google *Mozart* and *Jewish*, you will find some passionate speculations about whether or not he was Jewish. For some reason people seem to care about his ethnic origin. Should not the discussion be about the musician who authored a prodigious amount of great music? Would his achievements have been any less valuable if it was ever proved that he was Jewish? Is it not time to stop viewing ethnic identity as an indicator of value? The debate over Mozart's ethnicity illustrates the need to get past using racial categories as identifiers or descriptors in most every circumstance. Mozart's greatness needs to be appreciated for what it was, and what it is. In our time, many great achievements have been ignored or overlooked when accomplished by a minority group or a person of color. At one time American professional sports conducted business as though an entire race of people—African Americans—did not exist. In a bit of irony, African American athletes now dominate much of the sports scene. Mozart's abilities counter the idea that one musical style is superior to another. Our recent sports history should counter the theory that one group of people is superior to another too.

Ludwig von Beethoven

Ludwig von Beethoven is our final classical composer. Beethoven's career had two seasons of popularity, occurring about two hundred years apart. One period of fame arose because of his masterful use of harmony as he composed some of the most popular symphonies of the classical era. The other happened when he became the subject of a song, "Roll Over, Beethoven," popularized by twentieth-century rockers such as Chuck Berry and the Beatles.

One other point of interest about Beethoven was his ability to succeed while facing difficulty. Early in his life he had to overcome the tirades from an overbearing father who was convinced he would never amount to much. Later in life he lost his hearing, and despite an inability to hear, he was able to compose very complex music. Recently my friend Mike Lawrence performed a song by Joni Mitchell that brought to mind the period in Beethoven's life when he had begun to lose his hearing—particularly the words "take a walk, a park, a bridge, a tree."

The lyrics to the Joni Mitchell song above illustrate in part how Beethoven was able to create music, which is an auditory art form, without the ability to hear what he was composing. Beethoven was able to accomplish this by the use of musical memory and musical notation. Think back to our discussion of the overtone and harmonic series. The sequences found in each of them determine the spatial relationships that the notes will have with each other. They also explain why the predetermined relationship between notes will result in harmonies that are pleasing to the Western ear. Being that both of those series are immutable and often times cannot be heard, their relationship to each other in the series can be seen on paper. Once musicians are able to see their music on paper, they can then compose utilizing mathematical equations that will arrange notes in such a fashion to produce music. A logical question could be, how would a deaf person be sure that the selected notes blend in such a way that expresses that deaf composer's intent? Beethoven's life suggests that one answer could be found in the human ability to internally remember sounds independent of the ear.

Beethoven's deafness came upon him gradually. It is widely believed that Beethoven knew he was going deaf, and so he took precautionary steps to insure that he could continue to produce music. As the lyrics to Joni Mitchell's song illustrate, Beethoven would take walks in forests and visit the rivers near his home. He would study the sounds of birds and the sound of rippling water. This was all done in order to build a mental library of sound. Beethoven's library of sound enabled him to hear music, not in his ear, but in his head. It is fascinating that he developed the ability to write music without being near an instrument. Educator Patsy Stevens writes that Beethoven "liked taking long walks during the day. During these walks he planned his music. He would make notes in a notebook. Then in the evening after dinner, he would write music from about 7:30 to 10:00 p.m. He followed the same routine every day. If he was dining out and did not have his notebook with him, he would write on the back of a menu. Once he even wrote on a window shade."[14] How was all this possible?

Musicologist Daniel J. Levitin provides another piece of the puzzle related to Beethoven's unique composing ability. His best-selling book, *This Is Your Brain On Music*,[15] includes an illustration of a section of the brain found in the limbic system, called the hippocampus. It is believed that in the hippocampus, music is remembered, and musical experiences are contextualized. Most of us have from time to time sung a favorite song silently to ourselves, have we not? No one else can hear the notes we are singing to ourselves but they are very real to us as we sing them. Where did those

14. Stevens, "Ludwig von Beethoven," section, 8.

15. Levitin, *This is Your Brain on Music*, 271.

notes originate? Perhaps they are stored in the hippocampus to be accessed on demand.

Allow me to give you an example from the world of pop music. Earlier we discussed the basic blues/rock progression based on a simple chord progression that utilizes the one, four, and five chords. Remember that the chord names are taken from the scale tones found in the major scale. Once these chords are etched into the memory bank of a musician she or he can play thousands of songs with other musicians seemingly at the drop of a hat. This is possible because of the shared memory that millions of musicians have acquired by listening to, and playing, the same chord progression thousands of times. When a musician interacts with another musician that shares the same musical memory, they can play together with little or no prior rehearsal. This process is what is called jamming. The jamming process closely resembles the way people living in a particular culture can share attitudes and prejudices without ever having met each other.

The beauty of musical memory is that it allows for perfect note positioning to be achieved by picturing notes in a person's mind without the need for an instrument. Beethoven's napkin notation suggests that new ideas can be created in an instant, provided that there is a sufficient amount of data stored in the brain's cache. When I was a professional bass player, I was fluent in the vocabulary of a couple styles of music. Thousands of musicians were equally fluent in the same styles that I was, and they also understood the vocabulary. Because of this, I could fly from Los Angeles to New York, meet musicians for the first time, and we could play music together effortlessly. We could do this because we had a shared musical memory from which to draw. Let us now look at a hypothetical that illustrates my shared-memory theory—only this time in a negative context. Hopefully this will help us see the way shared memory can lead to trouble via false assumptions.

Picture this: a country music superstar who plays the fiddle, and a master violinist from the local symphony walk into a bar. Each notices that the other is carrying what appears to be a violin. They then assume that they are the similar type of human being because their skin is similar in color. They are in the same place, and they are carrying similar instruments, and they also believe that they are of the same race.

One says, "Want to play?"

The other responds, "Sure. What should we play?"

The first person says, "You play whatever you feel, and I'll do the same." Each proceed to play in a familiar style. They are both executing their style as well as it can be done, but the sound they are producing is absolutely horrible. How and why was the music so bad? After all, a violin and fiddle are the same instruments, and so that should not have been a factor. The musicians were equally skilled, even though their styles differed. Because their musical memory was not an actual shared memory, the music that they produced did not sound very pleasant, and neither of them had a good time.

Shared memory can be very beneficial to any group, but it can also cultivate negativity. It can be the glue that holds families, organizations, and entire countries together. Shared memory can also be a launching pad for striking out against each other. It is true that human beings are rational beings who are independent from each other. It is also true that human beings are organisms who share common genetics and traits that result in them exhibiting common behavioral patterns. For this reason we believe in the existence of predesigned inclinations toward specific characteristics embedded in our genetic makeup. We call that "human nature." Musicians who are raised in a musical family will typically gravitate towards a musical style similar to what their parents preferred. Is the preference for the parents' style of music a genetic predisposition at play, or an environmental influence? What if a third possibility exists? The offspring unintentionally absorb the preferences of their parents via a form of shared memory, and then later in life they believe those preferences to be innate? This shared memorization process could be how attitudes toward different people groups remain constant one generation after another. We tell ourselves that it is a natural instinct to prefer our own. The shared memory theory illustrates that we are not necessarily born with a genetic or environmental "preprogrammed preference chip" after all.

Beethoven intentionally memorized sounds that he believed would be useful to him in the future. Those sounds were then retained in his memory and available for instant recall. Similarly people on the inside of any particular social group, and people on the outside, each retain the not so flattering words said about the other for instant recall. When words such as *handicapped*, *disabled*, or (worse) *invalid* are used to describe a group of people over many centuries what would you imagine the result would be? The following quote explains how shared memory can easily become common understanding: "When a list of words, for example, needs to be memorized, the learner visualizes an object representing that word in one of the pre-memorized locations. To recall the list, the learner mentally "walks through" the memorized locations, noticing the objects placed there during the memorization phase."[16] If we use appearance to assign value to the people like my friends at The Refuge, then we run the risk of believing them to be of a lower value qualitatively, rather than simply different physiologically.

Allow me to illustrate another way that the shared-memory concept plays out in real life: Let us imagine that you are a white suburban business owner. You have never hired a minority in your life. You have not had much interaction with black people aside from the casual socializing that occurred during your school years. There are a few blacks that attend your church, and your relationship with them could even be described as warm. Suddenly for the first time in the history of your firm, you have a black male that had recently graduated from college on your payroll. Your expectations are that this employee should assume that certain tasks are part of his responsibilities, even though those tasks have never been discussed. At some point you observe this employee avoiding the tasks that you assumed were his responsibility. Because of shared memory in the form of negative stereotype, you interpret his inaction as poor work habits. Your conclusion is that what you have always heard is true, black males are lazy and not very industrious. What is not evident to you is that when you share your conclusion with others, it will soon become part of business culture's shared memory. Over time many of your colleagues will begin to believe the myths that circulate about black people too. Can you imagine what will happen when the next twentysomething black male applies at a business owned by one of your former colleagues in our hypothetical?

Together Forever

The classical era spanned four hundred years, and the three composers we have studied were linked together by style. Bach discovered polytonal harmony and the use of different chord structures to add color to his music. This fresh approach was passed on to Mozart, who took that and added to it. He then passed it on to Beethoven, all within the context of Europe's classical music community. In other words, even though they were completely different people who lived at different times, each of their lives had

16. Johns and Blake, "Cognitive Maps in Virtual Environments." section 2, para. 2.

an impact on the other. An African proverb says something to the effect, "I am because we are." This proverb suggests that regardless of what we do individually, it may only have value once it is viewed in the context of the larger community. That was certainly true for our classy classical composers, and I suspect it is true for us living today. We are all connected to each other whether or not we like that statement, or admit it to be true.

Classical music's popularity began to wane with the coming of the modern era. The composers that we have discussed should probably be viewed as the rock stars of their time rather than as highbrow stuffed shirts. That said, I would argue that a four hundred year run of popularity for any art form is a pretty impressive phenomenon. In the recent past, artists such as Leonard Bernstein, Arturo Toscanini, Luciano Pavarotti, and Yo-Yo Ma have enjoyed a modicum of popular appeal. However their popularity has not been on a par with that of many pop-culture icons. Classical music is more complex in structure than the average pop song of today. I believe it would be safe to say that it even requires more technical proficiency on the part of the musicians to execute. Even though I believe that is true, I am not saying that one should be viewed as better than the other, simply different.

Classical music's present level of popularity illustrates that there is nothing that is forever. At one time classical music was not only thought to be the superior style of music but the superior form as well. Although diversity existed within its boundaries, classical music was ordered around European (white) preferences, and so all other forms of music must by default be inferior. That pretty much characterizes the way our culture, and the evangelical church, is presently ordered, doesn't it? One set of preferences is simply accepted as the standard. The fact that classical music is no longer all that popular drives home the point that even what is of excellent quality may not always remain popular. Like classical music, another style of American music requires an equal amount of time and effort to become proficient technically. True to form, this music is not as popular as other simpler forms of music such as pop and rock. This music is not ordered from the white side in, but from the black side out. That music is jazz.

7

Jazz Is

To ask a musician to describe what jazz is may just be equivalent to asking a Christian what faith is. In both instances you will get as many answers as individuals asked. For this reason we should simply accept the reality that jazz just is, and it is an indescribable art form that originated in North America. *Wikipedia* begins one article on jazz the following way, "Jazz is a musical style that originated at the beginning of the 20th century in African American Communities in the Southern United States. It was born out of a mix of African and European music traditions. From its early development until the present jazz has incorporated music from 19th and 20th century American popular music. Its West African pedigree is evident in the use of blue notes, improvisation, poly-rhythms, syncopation, call and response, and the swing note."[1] To ask a jazz musician what jazz means, you would most often hear, "Freedom of expression."

I chose to open our discussion about jazz with this particular wiki quote for several reasons. The first is for the term *blue notes*. The blue notes that are referenced in the article are basically the same notes that Bach found himself in hot water over centuries before: flattened scale tones. Please think back to our discussion about scales and intervals. I said that when Mike and I flatted the third note of a scale in a Bob Marley song during a TOP session, a happy song became sad in the minds of the kids.

1. *Wikipedia*, s.v. "Jazz," line. 1

McGraw-Hill's Dictionary of American Slang and Colloquial Expressions says, "The word 'blue' can mean depressed and melancholy in certain contexts."[2] Jazz musicians made frequent use of the flatted, or blue-note, technique in order to elicit a specific emotional response from their listeners. There was a running joke about jazz musicians when I was involved in that community, that said, "Jazz musicians would rather flat their fifths than drink them." I would think that the originators of that joke meant it as a pejorative, and if so, it is illustrative of how worked up some can get over something so seemingly minor.

The writer of the *Wikipedia* article quoted above casually mentions that the origins of jazz stemmed from a mixture of European and African traditions.[3] I believe that observation to be worth exploring a little deeper. Some social scientists believe that mixing white and black populations is so difficult that it is close to being impossible to achieve. We are told that this type of mixing is in fact unnatural. The result of this perception is that most of the research done by social scientists is focused on learning *why* this is true, and not *if* this is true. For the record, I will stipulate that the social sciences do offer very important insights as to who we are and how we process life. However, what the *Wikipedia* writer said about the foundations of jazz leads me to wonder one thing: If jazz can successfully blend the black with the white in a musical setting, then why can we not do the same in a social setting? Moreover, if there exists a general acceptance that black and white populations cannot ever mix, why make the effort to learn why they cannot? If our society has become so comfortable with the social distance between black and white people, then maybe it is time for us to behave a little like Bach and the early jazz musicians. We should interrupt our complacency with a new and different sound or lifestyle—even if that new sound makes everyone a little uncomfortable in the process.

"When a Cat Don't Know, He Just Don't Know"

—ELLA MAE MORSE, JAZZ SINGER

Jazz got off to an inauspicious beginning related to its popularity level in America. One reason was that it was difficult for many music lovers to

2. Spears, *McGraw-Hill's Dictionary*, 37

3 *Wikipedia*, s.v. "Jazz."

understand its complexities, because jazz is about virtuosity. Another hurdle that jazz had to overcome was that some viewed it as a threat to white moral and cultural values. This perception was due in part to the fact that many jazz players were heavy drug users. For this reason many believed them to be poor examples for America's impressionable youth, especially white youth. Author Gary Gibbons had this to say about jazz in his book *Celebrating Bird*: "Jazz was considered to be a low art and was ignored by classical music critics."[4] Many of the initial concerns that swirled around jazz had to do with the root source of the music. That source was the African American community. However, even with all of the obstacles that jazz was forced to hurdle in its infancy, it did eventually grow into respectability as a genre. British jazz critic and author Alyn Shipton opines: "Of all of the musical styles to emerge in the 20th century, jazz was by far the most significant."[5] He goes on to say, "Jazz has only been truly popular music a few times in its history but its history is inextricably bound up with the development of popular music as a whole."[6]

Jazz comprises a wide range of subsets, and so today it may be difficult for us to grasp just how unique and revolutionary the music actually was at its inception. Please make a mental note that it may very well be impossible to pinpoint the time that jazz was born. It is probably wiser to simply think of jazz as an attitude or mindset that has always existed. That mindset is one that is desirous for freedom in all areas of life. As a musical style, jazz was chameleon-like in nature. The fluidity in the jazz approach to music happened because musicians could "jazz up" any existing musical form. The main ingredients necessary to produce good jazz appeared to be having the proper attitude, a fertile imagination, plus the physical dexterity needed to master an instrument. The key word in my last sentence is *imagination*. This is because jazz musicians are always striving to break free from rigid rules regarding form and structure found in most musical styles. They desire to expand the musical vocabulary by riffing over a wide variety of material. A *riff* is the name given to the note phrasing that a soloist or lead instrumentalist plays. It might be helpful to think of these as "mini-melodies." For this reason jazz riffs seem to be able to find a home in whatever musical genre they find themselves. Jazz musicians have the freedom to alter their notes to fit on top of the majority of Western musical forms.

4. Giddins, *Celebrating Bird*, 18.
5. Shipton, *New History of Jazz*, 1.
6. Ibid.

Today there are a wide variety of jazz styles available to us. Space will not allow me to cover every style. Using the vocabulary of my friends Robert and Kimberly, jazz contains "niches within the niche," meaning there are many subsets within the one genre. I mention this because in the early days people did not have access to a wide variety of jazz styles. This was because most of the early jazz players were basically poor and so they lacked access to the geographic areas where the larger venues were located. This limited exposure was a major impediment for jazz to be heard by a significant number of people. Radio was not as prevalent as it is today. Most black people, who were the primary audience for jazz music, were not fortunate enough to own a radio. Even if they did, the local stations played the music popular among white people. These factors, among others, are the reasons that it is very difficult to trace the history of jazz accurately. Even the birthplace of jazz is in dispute among historians. While most historians credit New Orleans as being the cradle of jazz, many credible historians cite Kansas City, Chicago, and New York as legitimate possibilities.

Jazz is noted for improvisation, experimentation, and innovation. How does this outflow of creative expression occur? In Greek mythology there was a goddess of music named Polyhymnia. That name, *Polyhymnia*, can be translated to mean "plural hymns" or "many songs." Just as the Greeks believed their goddess to be composed of many songs, the genre of jazz comprises many songs as well. What I mean by this is that jazz idioms are typically derived from preexisting songs and melodies. For example, during the golden age of jazz, musicians utilized the music composed for Broadway theatrical productions. Those songs were made into something new through the imagination and the creativity of the individual jazz musician. This method of creating music from other genres of music was new and fresh. Jazz is very much indebted to the musical forms of the past, and jazz musicians are equally indebted to the musicians that came before them.

Allow me to explain what I mean through the use of a personal illustration. At one point in my journey I made my living playing the bass guitar. During my career in music, I performed on jazz recordings as well as blues, rock, and funk. I developed the necessary skill to be asked to record through spending countless hours listening to bassists who were more proficient than I was. I studied the playing styles of people like Paul Chambers and Ron Carter from the Miles Davis band. I listened to my friend Richard Davis, who is also one of the most recorded jazz bassists ever. My hero for electric bass was Motown legend James Jamerson. I learned to play with power from Paul, and melody from Ron. I learned the use of chords and octaves from Richard, and syncopation from James. Over time the hours that I spent listening and learning did pay off. I became *me*, in the musical sense—meaning that I did develop a sound and style that others viewed as unique. This led to several record producers believing that my bass playing would enhance their product. My sound came into existence through the efforts and accomplishments of my predecessors. The ascendency of jazz to prominence in American music followed a similar track, and that track was building on the past.

A Fresh Wind

Louis Armstrong was born in New Orleans, Louisiana, just around the turn of the twentieth century. His life gave strong witness to a very creative spirit, and he was the first solo instrumentalist to become an international star. He achieved stardom even though he could not have come from a more socioeconomically challenged background. His personality exuded so much graciousness that many were unaware of the cruelty he had endured as a youth. When jazz was born, the division between black and white was wide and deep. This chasm existed because the South had managed to make the white/black divide the law of the land at just about the time that Louis was born. The stringent racial division that was legislated into law never lived up to the "separate-but-equal" nickname given to the policy. It appears the true reason the slogan was created was to make the oppressive Jim Crow laws appear to be consistent with America's cherished ideal of fairness. Gary Giddins writes about the early days of jazz: "The combination of Jim Crow racism and the public's inability to distinguish genuine achievement from meretricious imitation invariably favored exposure of white bands."[7] Later he adds, "In the United States, jazz was confined to gin mills and dance halls."[8] This sentence illustrates that the birth of jazz was difficult in its own right, but the black version of this music had to fight extremely hard to survive.

Let us accept as being true what the historians say who believe that New Orleans was the birthplace of jazz. Many of those same historians also believe that Louis "Satchmo" Armstrong was the founding father of improvisational jazz. It is amazing that this very high accolade was said to

7. Giddins, *Celebrating Bird*, 18.
8. Ibid.

be true of both his trumpet playing and his singing. However, I would put forth one caveat against labeling Armstrong the founding father of jazz in the broader sense. I would contend that the musician Scott Joplin be given some consideration as an important figure in jazz. He is at least a forerunner of jazz, if not an actual founder. Scott was a pianist who played a heavily syncopated style of music called ragtime. This type of music was popular just before jazz caught America's fancy, and many believe it to be a precursor to jazz. The following illustration may help you to understand why I see Mr. Joplin as such an important figure in music.

Imagine Louis Armstrong walking into a bar where Scott Joplin is playing the song "Alexander's Ragtime Band" without any accompanying musicians. Louis removes his trumpet from its case and begins to solo extemporaneously on top of Scott's rollicking piano. The music that the people would have heard in our hypothetical would have been jazz. Jazz is composed of free-flowing melodic improvisation in concert with chords and syncopated polyrhythm. This would aptly describe what Joplin's piano and Armstrong's trumpet would have created. Jazz can be anything, as long as it provides a vehicle for individual creative expression and it "swings."

Before going any further allow me to take a stab at defining the last word of the preceding paragraph. This will not be easy because the concept of swing could apply to many musical genres, and it is also entirely subjective. I will begin by asking you a question: Have you ever been involved in some type of activity with someone who you were not that familiar with? Of course you have! We all have. However, in this instance, imagine that the activity is difficult from the beginning: that it appears to be heading nowhere. Then something clicks, and the process begins to gel. Suddenly the activity has become easy, maybe even enjoyable. I believe that most of us have had a similar type of experience, have we not? We have even used familiar expressions to describe the phenomenon such as, "We finally got into the *swing* of things." Here is where that expression may have originated. During the jazz era when music would come together, and begin to gel, it was said to swing. In fact a popular jazz composer named Duke Ellington would later write a song titled "It Don't Mean a Thing (If It Ain't Got That Swing)."

Scott Joplin traveled extensively as an itinerant pianist playing his form of ragtime in "juke joints" all over the segregated south and beyond. Juke Joints were dance halls and bars that were frequently brothels. Solo pianists often provided the patrons with music that was very much a form of jazz.

What is of interest to our discussion is the racial makeup of the establishments that housed the ragtime piano players at the turn of the 20th century. Two similar entertainment venues were operating at the time. The venues frequented by white patrons were called "Honky Tonks." The black versions were called "Juke Joints." To create two distinct words to describe a similar thing by race speaks loudly about the attitude of many people at the time. They believed that black and white people were so different that it made sense to use different names for similar entertainment establishments. Even though many view white and black churches as being substantively different from each other, we do not invent completely different names for each one. This further highlights the arbitrary nature of unnecessarily finding difference in items that are essentially similar.

Let us now consider what life was like for African Americans at the time of the birth of jazz. In 1905 Robert T. Mott opened the first black owned theater in America, called the Pekin. It was located on Twenty-Seventh and State Streets in Chicago, Illinois, and it came to be known as the Temple of Music. The theater was an oddity for several reasons. First, it defied the widely accepted belief of white America that darker-skinned people were incapable of successfully operating a theater, or any other type of business for that matter. Second, the existence of the Pekin Theater dispelled the myth that black and white audiences could not attend and enjoy performances in the same building. Sadly, to overcome this perception, many believe that Robert Mott had to select a name for his theater that would not signal black ownership to whites. The good news is that the name did work, and it enabled Mott to skirt around the belief that the two groups could never be comfortable in close proximity.

The Pekin opened at the turn of the last century when rigid racial separation was expected in the churches of the day too. Today many churches still operate as separated entities via the principle of homogeneity in order to facilitate growth. This demographic-driven style stems from the belief that people feel most comfortable worshipping with their own. This then culminates with most religious practitioners accepting separate-but-equal churches as just the way it is. That is also the way it was then, at the time of the Pekin Theater. And to a degree, the way it is now.

John William Shaw, Catholic archbishop of New Orleans in the early twentieth century, said, "I, a Southerner, do not believe the good Lord ever intended that the races should fraternize."[9] The First Vatican Council stated

9. Bennet, *Religion and the Rise of Jim Crow in New Orleans*, 205.

that, "The church of Christ is not a community of equals in which all of the faithful have the same rights. It is a society of unequals."[10] At the time Louis Armstrong identified with the Roman Catholic tradition, and he must have looked at Christianity with a skeptical eye because of the way the Catholic Church was organized. Think about this: only white priests could serve or preach to black parishioners. That prohibition reflected the prevailing attitude of the time that blacks were not quite up to the task of leading. Black men were called boys by whites regardless of age in order to reinforce their supposed childlike mental capabilities. Perhaps this is why jazz musicians often referred to each other as "man" as a means of counteracting the indignity foisted upon them. The use of the word *man* as an interjection in much of black culture today is really not just a quirky colloquialism: it has significance.

Louis Armstrong was born into a society that viewed him as a substandard version of humanity, and the power of the United Sates federal government enforced that belief. Earlier in its history New Orleans had been one of the major players in the slave trade. Hundreds of thousands of darker-skinned people had been bought and sold on the very streets where young Louis would hone his musical skill just a few decades later. Louis Armstrong had what many would refer to as a traumatic or dysfunctional childhood. His father abandoned the family, and his mother turned to a life of prostitution. This resulted in young Louis being raised by his grandmother. However, there appeared to be some form of an entrepreneurial spirit lurking inside of young Louis because even at a very early age, he and his friends would sing for nickels and pennies on the streets of New Orleans. Mr. Armstrong's early years were tough and without much opportunity. He was left to fend for himself for the most part. Young black men had few educational or employment options in the post-Reconstruction South. But opportunity did knock on Louis Armstrong's door, and here is the way it happened:

> On New Years Eve of 1912, Armstrong fired his stepfather's gun during a New Year's Eve celebration and was arrested on the spot. He was sent to the Colored Waif's Home for Boys. There, he received musical instruction on the cornet and fell in love with music. In 1914, the home released him, and he immediately began dreaming of a life making music. While he still had to work odd jobs selling newspapers and hauling coal to the city's famed red

10. Ibid.

light district, Armstrong began earning a reputation as a fine blues player.[11]

It appears that Armstrong developed rapidly because he soon became skillful enough to replace the famed trumpeter King Oliver in the important Kid Ory Band in about 1918.

Please do not deduce from the preceding quotes that young Louis selected a career in music to the exclusion of other options that were available. Black people at that time were expected to perform the same menial work they had always done during the slavery years. The Civil War had decimated the New Orleans economy, and so everyone was going through tough times many years after its end. Additionally, Louis was born in the red-light district of New Orleans named Storyville and it was not exactly a hub of business activity. I would speculate that this environment went a long way towards teaching him to look to music as a means of hustling just to survive. As we look at some aspects of Louis Armstrong's life I ask that you attempt to see it through the lens that Louis used to see his world. Then try and understand why Louis chose to respond to that world in the way that he did. Finally, try to imagine the way that you might have responded given the same set of circumstances.

Once Louis reached adulthood he did not stay in New Orleans long. He was more than eager to escape the oppressive racism of the day. His first stop was Chicago, and it must have seemed like more of a reprieve that a relocation. In New Orleans young black males in particular were singled out for the worst of the worst kind of treatment. To illustrate how loathed and feared black males were at the time, "black men were barred from legally purchasing the services in either black or white brothels."[12] Presumably this ordinance was in place to insure that black males did not "pollute" or ruin the women for their white customers. One other possibility is that this ordinance was put in place to further strip young black males of their dignity. Maybe the ordinance was intended to humiliate them in order to achieve greater control. Whatever the reason for these prohibitions, they did not impair young Louis's ability to see himself as the artwork of God. He concentrated on becoming the person that he believed he could be, rather than a person deserving the treatment he received from white people.

A little later on there were many people involved in the pursuit of racial justice who felt that Louis's gregarious behavior undermined their

11. *Bio,* "Louis Armstrong," para. 4.
12. *Wikipedia,* s.v. "Storyville," section 2, para. 3.

demand for respect. They believed that his propensity to smile while enlarging his eyes when performing was an impediment to the appreciation of African American culture by the majority culture. The somewhat awkward paradox is that neither Louis's fame nor the behavior that got him in trouble with blacks seemed to exempt him from the same treatment that the less affluent blacks of the day received. In fact, when he did voice an opinion about the desegregation of public schools, Armstrong fell victim to strong white backlash. A *New York Times* commentator said this about the treatment Louis received after speaking out: "Mr. Armstrong was to pay a price for his outspokenness. There were calls for boycotts of his concerts. The Ford Motor Company threatened to pull out of a Bing Crosby special on which Mr. Armstrong was to appear. Van Cliburn's manager refused to let him perform a duet with Mr. Armstrong on Steve Allen's talk show."[13] Louis Armstrong joined the prophets depicted in Scripture that were persecuted for seeing wrongs and making an attempt to right them. Jazz and the community of faith have always needed a prophetic voice in order to insure progress. Louis Armstrong was one of those voices and another was our next jazzman, Charlie Parker.

The Yardbird Flies

Charlie "Yardbird" Parker was born in Kansas City, Kansas, but spent most of his childhood in Kansas City, Missouri. He was raised in a climate of racial discrimination, possibly heightened by leftover resentment from the bitter fights over slavery between Missouri and Kansas a generation and a half prior. Depression-era Kansa City must certainly have been a tough place to be young and black due to that lingering animus. The dehumanizing treatment of blacks that young Charlie more than likely experienced may have contributed to his drive towards excellence. Not being accepted by the world outside may have driven him inward. He probably retreated into that space in his psyche where there were few options other than tapping into a reservoir of creativity deep within. My understanding is that Charlie was driven by an internal desire (almost to the point of obsession) to succeed. He was so dedicated to his music that he supposedly referred to his music as his religion.

Charlie Parker came of age musically when jazz had settled down from the days when Armstrong and his peers were lighting up the country with

13. Margolick, "Day Louis Armstrong Made Nose," para. 14.

this new music via small combos. Sophistication had settled in, and jazz had become a form of popular music. This meant that people were dancing to it, and listening to it as background music for the script of their personal lives. This was the time historians refer to as the swing era. Large orchestras were formed, and they used prewritten charts to score their music in much the same manner as their classical predecessors had.

What Charlie Parker and his close friend trumpeter Dizzy Gillespie developed was not just a new way to structure and execute existing jazz forms. They brought a new approach altogether. Remember the joke about the flatted fifths earlier? Well, for the most part it was these two pioneers that popularized the use of that somewhat dissonant interval. The book *A New History of Jazz* speaks of the time period when Gillespie discovered the power of the flatted fifth. Dizzy was playing in a traditional jazz orchestra that was using charts to perform. Dizzy continually expanded the harmonic zone using these flatted fifths. One exasperated bandleader named Cab Calloway told Dizzy, "'Play what is written' . . .[,] describing his trumpeter's new ideas as Chinese music."[14] Mr. Shipton goes on to write that, "Dizzy's enthusiasm carried over to the other members of Calloway's band."[15] That happened because Dizzy had said, "I was excited about the progression and used it everywhere."[16]

I remember a book from the early 1980s that dealt with a theory about the existence of something called transpersonal communication. The basic premise of the book was that every human being has the ability to communicate with another without using any written or spoken words. Today most of us take for granted the concept of a nonverbal communication called body language. Many people believe that there is another way that people communicate without words—that is through the utilization of a form of intuition that is purely spiritual in nature. Charlie Parker and Dizzy Gillespie were "hearing" this new form of jazz, called bebop, without ever having met one another. The two of them came from different parts of the country, and yet they each were attempting to expand the vocabulary of music in much the same way. When the two finally began making music together it became apparent to each of them that they had somehow intuitively reached the same conclusion about the next direction that jazz was headed. Dizzy said this about their uncanny meeting of the minds, "I

14. Shipton, *New History of Jazz*, 444.
15. Ibid., 445.
16. Ibid., 444.

know he [Parker] had nothing to do with my playing."[17] Yet he would say later that "after we started playing together, I began to play, rhythmically, more like him."[18] It has been said many times over the years that "Bird" and "Dizz," as they were called, were so locked in musically that they sounded like one horn!

Jazz music is a very spiritual art form. The fact that these two giants could create similar ideas independent of each other is remarkable. It is a very good example of how humans are created as multisensory beings. Their music, and their relationship, also illustrates that human beings were created to create. A popular book a few years back put forth the notion that there was a subset of humanity called the "creative class." I disagree. I believe every piece of art that God creates, including you, is programmed with some type of ability to be creative. Your creative capacity may be lying dormant. Your closest friends may not even be able to see your gifts. In fact, you may even doubt their existence. Please put those doubts to bed, because I can assure you that those gifts are present.

Bird and Dizzy had to be confident that they were heading in the right direction because there is always an element of risk involved with exploring something new. They needed to muster the confidence to expose what they had created to possible criticism. Fear is probably what holds most of us back from venturing into the land of creativity. Fear is also the emotion that often prevents many of us from venturing into new and different types of relationships with people. Bird and Dizzy overcame their fears. I sense that we can too once we believe that the outcome will be of some value to us. Let us now shift our attention to one last saxophone player who earned a reputation for thinking outside of the box. I cannot emphasize strongly enough that John Coltrane did not just think outside the box. John Coltrane created a new box!

The Great Trane

John Coltrane was born in North Carolina and made his way north during the time Parker and Gillespie were leading the bebop charge in jazz. In fact, one pivotal moment for young "Trane" came when he heard Charlie Parker play at a club in 1945. John said of this occasion, "I'd come under the influence of Charlie Parker [and Dizzy Gillespie] . . . It was through their

17. Ibid., 449.
18. Ibid.

work that I began to hear about musical structures and the more theoretical aspects of music."[19] As with all art forms, in music new ideas frequently rise out of the ideas popular in the recent past. John Coltrane found the music of Bird and Dizzy to be masterful and challenging. As he did with most things in life, here John Coltrane had the eyes to see room for improvement.

The improvements he implemented would catapult Coltrane to being the titular head of the free-jazz movement. The platform for his ascendency to the top came as a result of an association with trumpeter Miles Davis. Davis was an established star in jazz. According to Coltrane biographer Lewis Porter in his book *John Coltrane: His Life and His Music*, Coltrane first joined Miles's group in September of 1957. In that book Miles is quoted as saying, "I have always wanted whoever played with me to find their own place in the music."[20] I think it is a safe assumption that Davis did not need to ask Coltrane twice to be experimental. Coltrane himself said of the time, "Miles is a strange guy: He doesn't talk much and he rarely discusses music. It is very difficult under these conditions to know exactly what to do, and so maybe that's the reason I wound up doing what I wanted."[21] The ethos of the artists across the entire musical spectrum during this time period was one of pursuing freedom and self-expression. Rock legend Jimi Hendrix once told me when he was looking for a bass player that if he needed to tell the bassist what to play, then that bassist probably was not the right person. This illustrates what the expectation was for musicians: you are free to play what you want, and so go for it!

Speaking of freedom, it was the concept of unbridled musical freedom that made John Coltrane famous. He and Ornette Coleman, in addition to a handful of others, are credited with being the architects of the free-jazz movement. Free jazz was an attempt to release musicians, primarily soloists, from the shackles of rigid rhythms and chord patterns. Here is one example of the lengths to which musicians of that era were willing to go in order to free themselves from the perceived shackles of standardized notation methods. My friend Leon Patillo recently reminded me that we once shared a stage with a band whose written arrangements consisted of simple cardboard cutouts that had been shaped into a square, a circle, a triangle, and so forth. The musicians were free to interpret those shapes in any way they desired and then play notes that corresponded with their interpretation of

19. Porter, *John Coltrane*, 42.
20. Ibid., 100.
21. Ibid.

the shape. That is how important freedom was to people caught in the wave of freestyle music: it was more important to be free than to play proper arrangements. Some jazz historians now write that John Coltrane did not go to that extreme, but fellow jazz saxophone great Archie Shepp recalls that at one recording session "the ensemble passages were based on chords, but then John put in the twist that, the chords were optional."[22]

Free jazz was the musical style that elevated John Coltrane's stature above that of the typical obscure jazz musician on the club scene in New York. Coltrane also desired freedom in other areas of his life at that time. His reign as king of jazz ran concurrent with the time period when it was both legal and socially acceptable to treat African Americans as inferiors. White Christian leaders viewed black people as being created for, and deserving of, their unequal treatment. That was the view of the average evangelical-church attender at the time too. Religion in America lagged behind the political institutions in the pursuit of racial equality. That was one reason why John Coltrane, and many other black jazz musicians, found the Nation of Islam attractive. Professor Lewis writes in his biography of John: "Many young blacks were turning to Islam in an attempt to find a church that is not white dominated. Some of them felt that Christianity had never accepted them as equals, even though they believed in Christ as fervently as any white person."[23]

Judging by how racially divided our churches are today, it is evident that things have not really changed all that much since John Coltrane's passing. My experience of working in several white churches is that there is not a lot of old-fashioned overt discrimination that occurs. However, there does seem to be a type of unwritten code among many white church leaders that says minorities are to be accepted but not be fully included. Notice that I said accepted and not welcomed, and it is especially true at the employment level. It appears that there is an undercurrent of suspicion and distrust about minority abilities, especially of black males, that frequently prevents open employment. The reason usually given for not hiring more blacks or other minorities is, we are not sure if you are a good fit. Part of the apprehension about hiring more minorities might be the same fear the people had about rock and roll. If blacks are visible on the platform then more blacks will follow. If that happens our church will no longer be a church for *us*. Not in 2015 you may be thinking. A popular nightclub in my city

22. Ibid., 263.
23. Ibid., 95.

THE ART OF GOD

does not stock a certain beer popular with blacks because they fear that if this beer were served, blacks would actually show up in large numbers. The idea of racial distance exists because many people like the concept of their race being the good one and the other suspect. Please consider that if jazz has taught us nothing else, it has shown us that notes once deemed to be discordant can and do fit together once they are allowed together.

The authors of *Being a Black Man* quote Duke University professor Mark Anthony Neal as saying, "The only thing [black people] could claim was their style."[24] The slave's attitude was, "I may not own my body, but I can make you look at me."[25] Therefore individual and cultural expression became just as important as the pursuit of freedom. African American jazz musicians such as John Coltrane found individual expression and freedom from musical constraints to be natural bedfellows. Rational thinking in both a musical and cultural context typically leads to the conclusion that what does not make sense must be bad and must be avoided. This conclusion might be wrong. Perhaps our time requires individuals who are both strong willed and visionary, like John Coltrane, to alert the broader community of creative possibilities waiting to be explored beyond what is presently accepted as sufficient.

A free-jazz band is a considerate community. A musician's participation in this type of band is not grounded in the idea of pleasing the self but in contributing to the group. I sense the majority of attempts to improve race relations are rooted in the idea that the dominant culture gets to play whatever note they desire as long as they are not doing violence to the minority group. The "play-whatever-note-we-desire" is a metaphor for the dominant culture's dictating which remedies are allowed in the process of reconciling races. The problem is that if the dominant tribe is allowed to determine what is and what is not violence or discrimination, the music that the races make will never be harmonious in any sense of the word. The beauty of the free-jazz model is that it only flourishes within a community of consideration. This is a community or band in which every participant is willing to adjust their attitude in order to advance the music (or to advance racial reconciliation). Advancement can only happen when every member's idea and contribution receives equal time and space to flourish.

24. Merida et al., *Being a Black Man*, 231.
25. Ibid.

86

8

Every Day I Have the Blues

Lorenza Ezell was a former slave whose recollections about the way life was on a Southern plantation were recorded in the excellent book *Voices from Slavery*. In the book Lorenza spins a gruesome tale recalling the inhumane treatment that people of African descent suffered at the hands of whites. He speaks of the long hours that the black people were forced to work. The prevailing view of white slave owners at the time was that slaves were not human, only property, and so they did not qualify for humane treatment. Since they were not human, slave owners concluded, slaves were not capable of creating real families. To the owners' way of thinking, slaves simply "bred" as a means of creating more "product" for the slave owner. As a result, generations of African people in North America lived and died without any self-awareness, let alone with any self-esteem.

Ezell says, "In dem days cullud people just like mules and hosses. Dey didn't have no last names."[1] Lorenza goes on to recall that his master was a Baptist preacher who allowed the slave families to attend church. Then Ezell recites some of the original gospel songs that the slaves would sing on Sunday mornings. Ezell's master was a minister, and this implies that he probably loved the Christian Scriptures. Additionally, the master was probably viewed as a moral person according to the standards of the day. Just think: neither the preacher's Christianity nor his morals prevented the

---

1. Yetman, *Voices from Slavery*, 112.

slave owner from treating other human beings so unethically. Is it possible for a person who believes in God to live in a harmonic relationship with Christ but not with other human beings? Looking back on Christian America's slavery days should teach us that the way we treat others says as much about our faith as the beliefs we profess to hold. The earliest forms of Christianity were not rooted in our concept of race. We should consider the fact that from a geographical perspective, Christianity was birthed at the intersection of Asia and Africa more so than on the paved streets of Europe. Non-Western Christians did have a concept of tribal affiliations, but they probably did not see different tribes as being the equivalent of separate races. A humanity divided by racial groups is antithetical to the unwavering love the Creator has for what was created. Today might be a good day for each of us to make a U-turn and to head back in the direction of a "raceless" Christianity.

Lorenza Ezell then switches gears and recites some songs that the slaves made up to describe life outside the church, meaning life as it really was. He says that, "before the war I was just big enough to drop corn and tote water."[2] He says that he was about eleven years old when the war started. This suggests that he came of age just as the institution of slavery was being dismantled. It must have been a time of uncertainty for the slaves. Just think: they had no idea if the war would result in their freedom, and they probably did not have any conception of what freedom meant anyway. However one thing was certain, regardless of the war and its outcome, life for African people was hard and would continue to be hard. It was against this backdrop that Ezell recalled some of the songs circulating among the slaves.

"My old massa run off and stay in de woods a whole week when Sherman [from the Union Army] come through. Dey a funny song us make up about him runnin off in de woods."[3]

> White folks have you seen old massa, up de road with he moustache on?
>
> He pick up his hat and he leave real sudden, And I believe he's up and gone
>
> Old massa run away, And the darkies stay home

2. Ibid.
3. Ibid., 113.

It must be now day Kingdom's comin,' And de year of Jubiliee[4]

Those words are about freedom and a new kingdom come—a kingdom on earth similar to the one that exists in heaven. These words also
underscore the mindset of many marginalized people. That is, they live a
life of unrealized and unfulfilled hope in the midst of misery. This song is
about life as it actually was for far too many innocent people. That song is
the blues!

There are many opinions about what *the blues* are, in both a musical
and sociological context, because the term is equally at home in both musical and sociological domains. Some believe the blues to be derived from
black gospel, while others see it as an amalgam of American folk music and
black gospel music. Some put forward the notion that blues music began as
a means of communication between slaves in the old cotton fields, utilizing
a style referred to as "field hollerin'" music.[5] Whichever way it started, the
blues were songs about how tough things were. I suspect there were also
a lot of backhanded encouragements in the somber lyrics, which said in
effect, "We are all experiencing this pain together, but we will get through
it together."

In my view, the point of the blues is that it is an honest expression
of a particular frame of mind. It is a type of commentary on whatever the
realities of life are at a given place and time. Given that blues music provides running commentary on life, blues artists care not only about the
specific words in a blues song but about the feeling behind the words—the
feelings the words evoke. It is not the bending of a guitar string that makes
music the blues. It is more than the amount of pain registered by the crying
phrases of a graveled-voiced singer. It is the emotion that comes from the
heart that makes this music called the blues so powerful and genuine.

There have been times when playing blues was a highly successful
enterprise for a fortunate few. A television talk-show host once asked electric blues superstar Jimi Hendrix if musicians that were making enormous
sums of money could really play the blues. Jimi's response was, "The more
money you make, the more blues you can sing sometimes." How can that
be? If the blues were in fact an outgrowth of hard times, would not the
accumulation of wealth automatically cancel the need to be blue? Certainly
that is one possibility. However, lack of financial resources is not the only

4. Ibid.
5. https://sites.google.com/site/generalbluesmc7/showcase/domain1v/.

challenge that people face in life. The lack of genuine acceptance by others can also be a contributor to the mindset of being blue. I would imagine that the state of being blue can and does affect everyone. No one is immune, and so everybody has at one time or another had the blues.

Many music historians believe that the blues came into being just before the United States Civil War. The melodic structure of early blues forms was of African origin, and the blues made use of the pentatonic (five-note) scale, which comes from the Celts. Again we can see that since its inception blues music was an amalgam of black and white musical styles. What is also important to our discussion is that the blues were a rural music, and for that reason many believe that the blues emphasized storytelling as much or more than music itself. Evidence for the importance of storytelling may be found in some of these lyrics written by the slave mentioned earlier, Lorenza Ezell:

> Early in the morning, Don't you hear de dogs a barkin? Bow, Wow, Wow!
>
> Hush, hush, boys, don't make a noise, Mazza is a sleepin.
>
> Run to de barnyard, Wake up de boys, Let's have the banjo pickin![6]

The blues also provided a momentary escape from the harsh reality of darker-skinned people's everyday existence. Singing this style of music can express both happiness and sadness simultaneously. It encourages a person to overcome rather than succumb to whatever the obstacle is that life presents. Put simply, singing a blues song can be helpful if for no other reason that it can really make a person feel good.

We Becomes Us

Most cultures have strong traditions of group singing. Some of this group singing is done for performance, while at other times it is done as a method of bonding. The choirs that sing in black churches across the United States are a perfect example of group performance and bonding. In times past, Negro spirituals would bellow out from simple church buildings: songs of solidarity, unity, and, most important, hope. The aspirations of hundreds of thousands of oppressed people were often articulated through the music that these choirs made. Gabriel Marcel wrote about this idea of a communal

6. Ibid., 114.

hope through song when he stated, "There can be no hope which does not constitute itself through a *we* and for a *we*. . . All hope is at bottom choral"![7]

I have read articles by psychologists stating that they believe there are other benefits derived from choral singing besides the enjoyment of participating in a musical performance. One possible benefit beyond the music component is psychological. As it applies to black choral singing in the church, it was a matter of release and relief. I am sure that what I am about to say will be understood by some, and it may offend others, but here it goes. I believe that some of the music that was sung by black church choirs was a form of the blues, only with Christian themes. There was an element of hardship in the lyrics of the songs that were called Negro spirituals. There was often a degree of pain expressed in the lyrics. There was also a cry for relief from that pain. All those emotions are "the blues"! The lyrics of the spirituals were often based on the Bible, but they also reflected the basic truths about an everyday lifestyle that was very hard. The lyrics were sung not only for entertainment and edification but for the ear of a compassionate God. However, it matters little if the songs were intended for the human ear or for the ear God: They were still a form of blues.

During the time period when the genre called the blues was young, juke joints and Christian churches were among the hubs of black culture. Remember that the term *juke joint* was slang for the nightclubs housed in barns, dilapidated residential properties, or storefronts reconfigured into drinking establishments to stage music. Black people lacked the resources to build fancy church buildings like those in the white community. For this reason black churches were sometimes formed using the same structures as the nightspots. Not only were the buildings often similar; there was carryover between the two in another way. You see, during the early twentieth century both entities were often populated by the same people. Yes, black people liked to party and they loved their church. The partiers would rock all night, and then roll in to church come Sunday morning. Please try to picture a skinny young fifteen-year-old—me—singing a popular blues song named "Stormy Monday Blues." I remember standing in front of my garage band in high school, dropping to my knees, then belting out lyrics that were written to expose the harsh realities of daily life for most working minorities. The song ends with a lament that says, Saturday night is the night to let frustrations loose before heading to church on Sunday to cry out for mercy

7. Quoted in Volf and Katerberg, *Future of Hope*, 172.

from God. The posture that I assumed to deliver the lyrics to that song was taken to emphasize the desperation that I felt the song expressed.

Perhaps it was the sheer honesty of the lyrics that caused them to have such an impact on me. Whatever the reason, they touched me very deeply. Consider the way that the songwriter views the workweek. The very title "Stormy Monday" evokes a mental picture of the violence and disorganization that a storm causes. Having once lived in Florida's hurricane alley, I can assure you that a stormy Monday is not a pleasant metaphor at all. Notice that the cry at the end of the last paragraph was for mercy and not relief. It is not an escape from the realities of life that the blues seek. The desire is for God to mercifully give the strength to overcome whatever life brings.

Workingman's Blues

Fats Domino recorded a song prior to the release of Bobby Blue Bland's version of "Stormy Monday" named "Blue Monday." The lyrics on Fat's recording of "Blue Monday" likely expressed the way black people felt as they worked in their lowly positions. The takeaway from this song was that Mondays were blue because certain people had to work the entire day like slaves of old. During my teen years black people referred to their jobs as "a slave." If I had asked a friend what he was doing on the upcoming Monday, he most likely would have responded, "I'll be at my slave." What he would have been saying was that he was at his place of work.

When I was training to become a pastor, we were taught that we needed to understand what motivated those we counseled, and what it was that gave them a sense of self-worth. Many psychologists have theorized that the majority of people (that is, men) get their significance from their occupations. These psychologists offer as proof that in small talk Americans frequently ask, what do you do? upon meeting someone for the first time. For these psychologists, that this question prevails in small talk demonstrated that we Americans place considerable importance on our jobs.

Jobs may have been important to white people, but they were not equally important for blacks. Black people often viewed their jobs as drudgery—and rightfully so, because drudgery is exactly what they were in most cases.

The pessimism expressed by some of the blues songs was not necessarily about having to work for a living. No, the "lazy black" stereotype was for the most part a very convenient myth. Just think how much work was expected from blacks when they were slaves and later as sharecroppers. If you have ever worked in a field during the very hot summer months, you would know not to characterize anyone who actually did this type of work as lazy. The work schedule held by the vast majority of black people was not your typical office hours. Quite the contrary, for black people, work meant performing backbreaking labor in the field from dawn to dusk six days a week. A privileged few were allowed to toil nonstop in an employer's home six days a week. My grandmother was one of those privileged few. She was a live-in housekeeper, and I am sure that broke my grandmother's spirit—as well as my father's heart.

The ambivalence that some black people expressed towards their jobs may have been more about the type of work that was available to them, and less about the thought of working hard. Being restricted to the jobs that the majority of whites would not do automatically signaled second-class status. When I was growing up, the perception among my peers about job prospects echoed something Solomon said about many secular pursuits in the Bible. He refers to them as meaningless. The truth is that a starter job for one group (whites) was frequently the job ceiling for another group (blacks).

Some people perceive that we live in a meritocracy, and success comes as a direct result of hard work rather than as a result of other factors—such as access to opportunity. This perception is often wrong, regardless of how firmly embedded the idea is. The charge that inequality exists in the work-place is warranted, and unequal access to opportunity is certainly one of the culprits creating this imbalance. Consider this: Many black males are viewed with suspicion whenever they venture out of their own neighbor-hoods, especially if they are young. Our news media has done a very good job of implanting the idea into the public that these young people are auto-matically thugs. Young black men are especially thought to be thugs if they "dress black"—whatever that means. Some white people will justify their negative attitude toward black people through the use of crime statistics or through personal anecdotes.

I cannot tell you how many "stuck-in-a-bad-neighborhood" stories I have heard from white people over the years. Let me share one of them with you, just to give you an idea of what they sound like, and of how prevalent they are. Two years ago I was sitting around a table of white pastors discuss-ing my first book, *A Story of Rhythm and Grace*. One pastor opined that it was perfectly reasonable for a white person to be cautious, if not fearful, if in a black neighborhood. I pressed a little to find out why he was so sure that this was true. He then related the following story: He recalled a time when he had gone to visit his grandmother in another city. Once he had arrived, he decided to drive her to do some errands. He did not grow up in that city, and so he was not very familiar with the different areas. He said that his grandmother's car had broken down in one of those "not so good areas." He called his insurance company to send a tow truck. While he and his grandmother were waiting for the truck, they locked their doors and did not get out of the car. He said that several black males had walked by, and some had even stared at them with menacing looks. He concluded by saying that he was very uncomfortable, and that he was never so happy to leave an area in his entire life.

I accepted the story as being true, but I did press him just a little to make sure his perception was accurate. I asked him to tell me exactly what the young men did to make him feel so uncomfortable. He said that they did nothing other than stare at him and his grandmother. I asked if they said anything to him. He said that they had not said one word. I asked if anyone from the neighborhood had approached the vehicle, and he said they had not done that either.

I said, "If they did not speak to you, and they did not take any steps towards your vehicle, how do you know they were not curious about whether or not you needed help?"

The pastor then admitted that it never occurred to him that darker skinned people would be willing to help him. He admitted that he had assumed that the men's stares had signaled that the men were deciding whether or not it was worth robbing this pastor and his grandmother in broad daylight.

I am confident that this type of unease carries over into the workplace and into most other public spaces as well. I believe that it is impossible for some employees to not experience discomfort when they are working with people that they are not accustomed to being around. Think with me: Of all of the senses that we possess, is not sight the most depended on, and therefore the most important? In both business and church culture we utilize *vision* statements to educate people about the organization. We accept adages like "seeing is believing" as reasonable and true. We intentionally dress in a certain fashion for our jobs to ensure that our appearance is appropriate. We do this because we want our employers to *see* us in a favorable light. But some features of our appearance are permanent. One such feature is our skin color. What happens if our skin color makes others with a different skin color uncomfortable around us? What happens when those "others" just referenced are the very people in whose hands our future rests? Even though we use our eyes to evaluate most everything in life, when it comes to skin color many insist that they can simply turn their eyes off and become "color-blind." I think not; and besides, what if the different skin colors were designed for our enjoyment? Would it not be wiser to develop a taste for them instead of developing blindness to them?

Blues in the Key of See(ing)

Imagine that each of the following scenarios is actually true. It is eight o'clock in the morning in San Jose, California. A group of teenagers decide that they would rather drive south to the beach town of Santa Cruz than attend their classes. They get someone to buy them a couple of six-packs of beer, and they are ready to party. The young man driving has the appearance of a stereotypical California surfer, in that he had that muscular, blond athletic look surfers are known for. The beach is located about thirty miles to the south of their school. To get there they must drive a very windy road named Highway 17 that cuts through the Santa Cruz Mountains. The driver is barely exceeding the posted speed limit, but the speed is enough to catch the eye of a California Highway Patrol officer. She pulls them over and notices a small amount of marijuana on the floorboard. Then she spots open beer containers in the backseat. Later in the stop she notices that the driver has the last name of a prominent San Jose businessperson. She inquires if they are related and the kid says, "Yeah, that is my dad." She issues them a stern warning about their irresponsibility by ditching school, speeding, and having both drugs and beer in their vehicle. She confiscates the little baggie of marijuana, has them empty the beer cans on the roadside, and sends them on their way.

Now let us look at another scenario. A group of black inner-city kids are eating lunch at their school across town from the kids in our first example. They decide that they have had enough school for the day. Because it is an extremely hot day, and the school year is almost over, they decide to skip school and head to Santa Cruz. They find someone to buy them a few six-packs of beer, and off they go. As soon as they begin driving on Highway 17 a set of red lights begins to flash behind them. As fate would have it, the same officer that pulled over our first set of truants has just stumbled upon another set. She walks up to the driver's window and notices that the driver's hair is not blond this time but black. Not only is it black, but it is styled in dreadlocks. Dreadlocks are the braided hairdos that Bob Marley popularized in the 1970s. Not only does the driver have dreadlocks, but he also has an armful of tattoos. The officer's eyes make it over to the passenger seat and settle in on a young black male wearing a hoodie. (That is a hooded sweatshirt that many assume signals gang affiliation when the kid wearing it is black.) The officer spots an open container of beer in the backseat, giving her probable cause to initiate a search. Once she has all of the passengers handcuffed, she finds a small baggie of marijuana in the pocket of a passenger. She then calls for backup and arrests them all.

Unequal treatment within our justice system is quite common, but it is not one of the problems high on our current lists of societal ills. Nevertheless, a double standard does exist in our justice system along racial lines, and it has its roots in the way the majority culture sees minorities. The officer viewed the first group of high schoolers as good kids who were simply off track. The officer may have viewed the second group of high schoolers as future thugs in need of stern treatment in order to keep them from becoming worse.

Systemic injustice as shown in the example above is what creates the blues for an entire community. Do not think for one moment that the stories about one group getting away with it and of the other group being arrested will not make the rounds within their respective communities. However, when the stories are told, there will be two different reactions to them. When the kids at the white school hear the story from their peers, it will elicit fear in their minds. They may process the event as a warning about stepping outside the lines of proper behavior. They will see the possibility that one bad choice could ruin their promising futures. Sadly, the peers of the black kids might view the story told at their school as just further proof that they cannot catch a break. So the story of the black kids going to the beach will provide yet another reason to be blue.

Our justice system is bogged down due to the weight placed on it by the laudable ideal of equal justice for all before the law. The biggest problem is that the presence of inequality in the justice system is a complex issue. There are no simple answers to the question, what should we do? To illustrate how difficult the task of doling out equal justice can be, let us build on the last hypothetical. Let us imagine a young white judge who believes that most of the criminals behind bars deserve to be there. He is selected to hear the case of the young man with the dreadlocks. This young man is an above-average student. He is involved in athletics in school and is a regular church attender. The judge actually likes the kid, and after speaking with him the judge decides that he is going to "help" him. This help comes in the form of probation. The judge's thinking is that the student seems to be a good kid, and probation might scare him straight. Of course at this point in the case the judge could have given the kid a stern lecture, and then could have sent him home in the same way that the surfer kid had been, but the judge chooses not to.

What happens is that two weeks later our young man is a passenger in another car that is stopped. A person in the front seat panics and then places a small amount of marijuana under the seat in front of our dreadlocked kid. The police find the marijuana and assume that our young man had placed it there to avoid arrest. Now our young probationer is right back in juvenile court facing a different judge. The new judge notices that this is his second arrest in a month and believes that his bad behavior is escalating. In her heart she believes that he is on the road to becoming a thug. Since our young man just turned seventeen a week prior, the decision is made to try him as an adult. He is found guilty of possessing an illegal substance and sentenced to six months in jail. He is now a convicted felon who can neither vote nor take part in government programs designed to help low-income people. His ex-con status will disqualify him from being a candidate for any meaningful employment. This story will not end well! There is a high probability that a dismal outlook on life could develop in the heart of our young man over the next ten years. This outlook could lead him to become a repeat offender on the road to homelessness. The sad part is that this entire chapter of this black youth's life is written this way only because the original arresting officer saw two identical scenarios—one involving white teens, and one involving black teens—and processed the second scenario in a different way from the first based on the skin color of the second set of (black) teens.

Three Chords and the Truth

As I stated earlier, the chord pattern for the blues is simple. The vast majority of blues music is based on just three chords. The three chords are the one (I), the four (IV), and the five (V) chords. One detail about the five chord is particularly interesting and germane to our discussion. Earlier I mentioned that at one time the Rolling Stones were my favorite band, and for consistency's sake I will use one of their recordings to illustrate my point here. They recorded a song titled "Heart of Stone" on one of their early albums. The opening chord of the song is very unusual for a blues introduction. Remember that we discussed chords and chord patterns earlier? Traditionally, a blues song will begin on the root chord (the one chord). However, "Heart of Stone" begins on the five chord, and the five chord in this instance is not a simple triad (a three-note chord). The chord used in this song is a five (V) chord with a minor seventh note added on top of the triad. The note is written like this, D7, if you are in the key of G. In this instance the D7 chord would become the five-dominant seven because of its relationship to the root chord, G.

Allow me to break this concept down a little. In the key of G the D7 chord consists of the notes D, F#, A with an added C. The third note in that D7 chord, or the F#, is the seventh note in a G-major scale. This causes the F# to be the primary leading tone because of its location one half step below G. When the seventh note above the five chord's root is played (in this case the C above the D), the C becomes a secondary leading tone. (The two notes called leading tones, when they are used in a chord progression can lead the listener to desire that another chord be played to resolve tension.) Just think: two notes, F# and C, placed in a certain position within the chord, can cause most listeners discomfort until another chord is played. When the chord that eases that discomfort is played, it is called a resolution. In our example, the D7 called for the playing of a G to bring resolution, and that is exactly what the Stones did in their song "Heart of Stone."

To summarize, leading tones automatically bring with them a degree of tension, and that tension will linger until it is resolved through some type of action. Racial tensions are often due to the poor placement of people groups in relationship to each other. The cultural dominant seven chord is not seeking resolution, and it results in lingering tension. Metaphorically speaking, when racial tension exists, people need to look for some form of social leading tones—ideas that genuinely lead towards unity—not just to relieve the tension but to bring resolution. Continuing with our metaphor, note that in our example two notes would bring resolution. The secondary leading tone was farther from its resolving tone than the primary tone was—one whole tone versus one half tone. By analogy, the distance between people could be a factor in how quickly resolution will be achieved. When we are planning methods for bringing people together, the way requiring the fewest steps to close the social distance should probably be considered best.

These Blues Have Got to Go

Today most people seldom engage in conversations about their attitudes concerning race. People are becoming less and less comfortable verbalizing their true thoughts and feelings about their positions on race. If a circumstance should arise that forces people to engage, then engagement often happens in shouting matches or in name-calling sessions. In our previous example when the "five-dominant seven chord" (V7) is resolved by another chord, relief, pleasure, and satisfaction come to the listener. I am confident that a similar outcome would occur in race relations if we ever got to the place where resolution, instead of isolation, was a goal of the majority of people on all sides of the issue. Please remember that it was the uncomfortable feeling that the leading tone produced that caused the resolution to become a welcomed sound. Today a great many people are too comfortable living in their isolated and self-segregated communities to see the need for resolving the tensions that are the result of that lifestyle. People hardly ever remain in their space or their side of town 24/7, and when they do venture into the other's turf, they are uncomfortable. I once invited a young Latino man who lived on the East Side of Austin to our predominately Anglo church on the West Side. He politely declined, and the reason he gave me was that he felt he needed a passport to travel to that other side of town. That hurt me and made me sad, but then again I understood.

Tension between people who are not in harmony with each other cannot be resolved unless they are willing to admit there is a problem. Resolving tension cannot occur until people rid themselves of their indifference towards each other. I am thinking in terms of being indifferent to any form of injustice foisted upon people outside their own particular group. (Think of the kid with dreadlocks in the story above) People love to hide behind platitudes such as, Things are not perfect, but they are certainly better than they were in the past. I believe that to be the vocabulary of apathy. When we mouth those words, is there any deep thought given as to how things are better, and better for whom? Our individualistic culture views the prospect of pursuing something that benefits others rather than our own desires as complete foolishness. We would rather endure the discomfort that racial tensions bring than seek to resolve those tensions, if the resolution comes with a cost. The number of wars that Americans have fought indicates that we understand that freedom comes with a cost, but for some reason we recoil from the notion that racial peace would also have a cost.

9

Dotted Lines

Having briefly discussed country music earlier I want to begin this chapter with a confession. I am a recovering country-music hater! Yes, there was a time in my life when I absolutely abhorred country music and all it stood for—at least I thought I did. I believed that I had nothing in common with anyone who longed for the good old days of the Confederacy and segregation. In my view at that time, the genre of country music was home to some of the most insular people in America. Its battle lines (so to speak) appeared to have been drawn around conservative politics and racial segregation. I also believed that country-music listeners and the musicians who made it had very little interest in the world outside their inward-focused subculture. If you liked pickup trucks, guns, two steppin', and barbecue, you were in; if not, good luck! Here's confession number 2: I presently live in Texas and drive a truck, and while I do not own a gun, I love barbecue: so much for the wisdom of holding onto prejudices built on stereotypes.

Early on, the style of music we are discussing in this chapter was called *country and western*. In the 1960s country purists believed that Elvis had killed country music. Purists in the 1970s believed that Willie Nelson, Waylon Jennings, and Johnny Cash had done the same. Country music did begin to diversify in the 1990s and 2000s, and if any purists remained during that time frame, it appears they finally threw in the towel. At present, country music seems to be at peace with itself, and it has learned to be accepting of the many different styles within its borders. Most country aficionadoes believe that the music they listen to, whether it is honky-tonk, bluegrasss, or Texas swing, is still country music. In many ways this "accepting diversity within the one" illustrates the underlying premise of this book as it relates to the human family. If you are part of the human family, then you are the artwork created by God: this is true regardless of your physical abilities or your physical appearance.

Folk music is a name given to music that expresses the perceptions and perspectives being lived out by people within that distinct culture. Folk music's lyrics are typically derived from the everyday experiences common to all within one particular subset or subculture. For example, one of the regions where country music established roots was Appalachia. According to the online source *Wikipedia*, "Appalachia is a cultural region in the eastern United Sates that stretches from the southern tier of New York State to Northern Alabama, Mississippi, and Georgia."[1] It is a region of the United States that is typically home to a great number of people who are lower middle-class and uneducated. In fact, people living outside the region coined the term *hillbilly* to identify the people from the region.

The term was meant to be a pejorative because hillbillies were believed to be lazy, ignorant, and poor. In a bit of irony those three descriptors (i.e., lazy, ignorant, and poor) were also used to describe people thought to be from a very different race: blacks. However, the irony does not end there. You see, many believe that the music that originated in that region was a blend of British folk music and "ethnic" music of Caribbean slaves. It is interesting that the same ingredients musicologists believe were used to create country were also used to create the blues. Appalachia was home to people who lacked education and so most of what we know about the music's origins comes to us through oral history. But one thing is certain: if country music did have one single geographic area responsible for its origins, Appalachia would be a very good choice.

If the blues were the roots music for much of black America, then country music filled that same role for a large segment of white America. Therefore, from both a musical and cultural standpoint the blues and country are closely related. It is amazing how much animosity has existed between poor Southern whites, and Southern blacks over the years,

1. *Wikipedia*, s.v., "Appalachia," 1.

considering they had shared very similar life experiences. One would think that having so much in common would make each group sympathetic to the other. Unfortunately that is the problem with the way we have always done race relations: we dislike first, and if any reasons emerge for why we should change our perception, we ignore them

A guitar player that I played with in the Buddy Miles Band, named J. P. Cervoni, had a saying that he would often repeat in jest: "You work hard and then you die." J. P. used that expression to say that rock-and-roll musicians may as well live for today because the next gig (job) was not promised. That saying also illustrates what life was like for both the black and white rural poor during the formative years of each of the musical genres that we have been discussing. When I was a preteen there was a country song that became popular on the pop charts expressing much the same sentiment. It talked about what life was like for coal miners in Appalachia. It appears they had a system in place where the worker's did not get paid in cash from the mining company but received vouchers instead. The song was about the fact that you could work all week but still owe money to the company at the end of it. The name of the song was "Sixteen Tons," and it was written by guitarist-singer Merle Travis.

The fact that it was Merle Travis who wrote that song of lament about life in rural Appalachia was of interest to me personally. You see, I grew up with a guitarist named John "Sonny" Glaze. At one point he became a fan of the country guitarist Chet Atkins. It was Chet who popularized a method of playing a guitar called "Travis picking." If you guessed that the playing style was named after the writer of "Sixteen Tons," then you guessed correctly. But there is another reason why that song's author was of interest to me. Do you remember at the beginning of this chapter that I confessed to being a recovering country-music hater? People in recovery say that recovery is a process, and very often a long and hard process at that. Today I am becoming more and more appreciative of the many styles of country music. Here is how this process began.

Sonny, who is white, and I were in a band together called the Project. I noticed that Sonny would often play his guitar fingerstyle instead of using a pick. Guitar picks are the small triangular objects that guitarists hold between their fingers in order to strum the strings. What Sonny did was place the pick in his mouth, and then he would use his thumb and remaining fingers to pluck the strings. This style fascinated me, and so I asked where he learned it. He told me that he had learned "Travis picking" by watching

Chet Atkins on television, and that a lot of country guitarists used it. Suddenly I had a problem. How was I to pursue this technique if I had to get it from musicians who were playing a style of music that I disliked? I had to choose between letting go of my interest in that style of playing, or letting go some of my distaste for the people making the music. Thankfully I chose the latter. Before we move on to discuss country music and how it fits into our discussion about God's art, please remember that I only disliked country music for no other reason than I did not like it. Have you ever felt the same about something or someone? If we are honest with ourselves, then we know we have all done that at one time or another. However, it does become a problem when we allow ourselves to feel that way about people.

The decision to follow Sonny's lead forced me to listen to some country records that featured guitarists who were using the Travis-picking style. Through this process I learned that the pursuit of common interests would naturally construct bridges that are not that difficult to cross, should one choose to do so. My friend and I did pursue that method of guitar playing together, and thankfully I did take a step into a musical environment that I had always believed I disliked. My willingness to let go my prejudice had a practical benefit because it helped me to develop a method of playing that I use to this day. It was music that brought Sonny and me together, and it provided a useful tool for my career advancement. Many opportunities are available for you to achieve similar results revolving around every human interest imaginable. People can and will come together when the focus is off of the perceived difference and redirected to whatever it is they have in common. Commonalities are present whenever people are together; the key is to recognize and then pursue them.

Pickin' and Choosin'

Like it was with the blues, any attempt to put forward one definite time when, or place where, country music began is impossible. To make the effort to isolate one influential person to credit as the progenitor of the music would be futile as well. For example, a singer named Big Bill Monroe had an entire style named bluegrass credited to him mainly due to his being raised in the Bluegrass State, Kentucky. He was definitely a true pioneer, and yet he was not really the father of country music. There are far too many artists that have made major contributions to the development of this style of music over the years to select just one as the most influential. For that reason I have selected five individuals, and one family, to be the focus of our discussion. They are Jimmie Rodgers, the Carter family, Hank Williams, Charlie Pride, Willie Nelson, and Garth Brooks. I selected these six artists because each of them has helped shape trends within the genre, and they brought fresh ideas to country music.

Jimmie Rodgers

At the time of writing, Jimmie Rodgers's website welcomed its visitors with the following statement: "The Father of Country Music has had a profound impact on all of our lives and touched our souls with his simple but unique way with music."[2] The mention of Big Bill Monroe was my way of letting you know that I am aware that many have argued that he was the true father of country music. Others argue that the father of the music was Jimmie Rodgers. If Jimmie Rogers was not the true progenitor of the genre, he surely was country music's first superstar. In 1927 Jimmie Rogers recorded a song named "Blue Yodel No. 1," also known as "*T* for Texas." That song sold enough to make Jimmie a household name and a legitimate star in the U.S.

Here's a side note: the word *blue* in the title could very well be a reference to the musical style that was so prevalent in the black sections of towns across America. One other interesting detail about Jimmie's first hit was how far-reaching its influence was to become. His yodel later influenced another country giant named Hank Williams. I have a friend named Danny Brooks, and he is a blues singer from Canada. I occasionally play bass with him when his regular bassist is busy elsewhere. When I play with Danny, we mostly play the songs that he has written. The majority of the songs we play come from his most recent release titled *Texassippi Soul Man*. Danny was born just about twenty years after Jimmie died, and about twenty-five years after "*T* for Texas" was a hit in America. Jimmie's song "Blue Yodel No. 1" was renamed because of its opening line: "*T* is for Texas, and *T* is for Tennessee." Danny wrote a song titled "Trouble Me No More." That song begins with the following lyric: "*T* for the tears that I cried over you, / *T* for the trouble that I know you put me through." Can you see how Jimmie's hit could have had both a cross-cultural and cross-generational influence on a young songwriter? I find it fascinating that when it comes to art and music,

2. Jimmierodgers.com/, "Home."

differences such as race, age or disability, and even geography do not always lead to separation.

Speaking as a pastor, I wish that I could make that same statement about our churches. However, from my observations this is still a very long way from being true. Perhaps if the church could accept a more artistic vision of the world around it, then things could improve. What I mean by "artistic view" is this. Artists tend to see the beauty in most everything and everybody. Many of our churches believe that pointing out people's flaws, moral failings, and other aspects of their lifestyles to be its assigned duty in society. Artists are intentional about seeing the beauty in everything, including imperfections. Yes there is a beauty present even in things we label imperfect. Remember the Refuge? The fact of the matter is this; Christians should see the beauty in everyone, and everything, because it honors God to do so. The Christian tradition presupposes that all humanity is inherently flawed to varying degrees anyway, and so there is no quality of perfection in people. Additionally, the Spirit of grace that is alive inside of every Christ-follower should enable each one to see the beauty in all that has been created. That is the way grace looks and sounds, and that is what grace actually is. This is because most of what we see, related to people, is still being created, and people are an extension of the Creator. If a person chooses to dislike what was created, it might naturally follow that person is choosing to dislike the Creator. Put another way, if you value the artist, it should result in an earnest effort to see some value in the art produced by that artist.

The Carter Family

At about the time that Jimmie Rodgers's music was taking America by storm, another important musical entity was coming into prominence. This time it was not a lone singer with a guitar but a family of singers and "pickers." (A picker is another way of saying guitar player in country-music vernacular.) The family included mother Maybelle Addington Carter, who played guitar and sang harmony and Maybell's brother in law, A. P. Carter, who played fiddle and sang bass. A. P.'s wife, Sara Carter, was also part of the group. She played autoharp and sang lead vocals. A. P. appears to have been a bit of a visionary regarding race relations and reaching out to people living with disabilities. He met a black guitarist with disabilities named

Lesley Riddle. They not only wrote songs together, but they became very close friends.

I just finished listening to Mr. Riddle sing a song called "John Henry." What caught my ear was the similarity in musical style between the white Carter family and the black Mr. Lesley. It further strengthens my hypothesis that music was crossing racial boundaries long before physical bodies followed suit. Music is spiritual: it speaks to the mind, heart, and soul. It may very well be that because music is a multisensory medium, it does not really break down barriers as much as it blows right past them.

The Carters' music continued the trend of the lyrical content of country music expressing the realities of life as understood by working-class, white America. Just as blues songs touched on the working conditions of blacks, so country lyrics frequently dealt with the harsh conditions the white working class endured adjusting to the rapid changes of post–World War I America. Appalachian whites, and many others, suffered economically through the 1920s due to the agricultural failures that resulted from a severe drought. This put poor whites and the children of former slaves in similar economic positions. The lyrics in blues and country often express both lament and hope. The music demonstrates that whites and blacks were not as far apart as they believed themselves to be. They were actually within a few words of each other. Notice how the Carter family's first hit is illustrative of that writing style. Here is the first verse and chorus of their initial major hit, recorded in 1928, titled, "Keep on the Sunny Side." Notice the positivity that is expressed in the Carter recording of a traditional American folk song:

> There's a dark and troubled side of life,
>
> there is a bright and sunny side too
>
> Tho' we meet with the darkness and strife,
>
> the sunny side we also may view.
>
> Keep on the sunny side, always on the sunny side,
>
> Keep on the sunny side of life![3]

Can you see how white roots music often contains a positive outlook that is built into its lyrics? Now contrast that with the black blues tradition. In the black blues idiom, the Lord is looked to for a rescue from whatever it is that is pressing down on the people. Remember the "Lord have mercy"

---

3. pdinfo.com/, s.v., *Public Domain Songs*: "Keep on the Sunny Side," no. 4.

cry that I sang, from "Stormy Monday" in the previous chapter? Whites are able to look within themselves for comfort and encouragement because their shared story is one of overcoming the tyranny of the British Empire, and then settling the land. The organizing myths created by these troubadours not only told the story of this new nation but they penciled in a can-do undertone that buttressed the idea of American exceptionalism. For this reason there has always existed an almost providential expectation in white American culture that everything should be okay in the future. This belief is reflected in the lyrical content in much of country music.

That type of optimism was not always present in the lyrics of black roots music, and this is one area where the similar musical styles diverge. In the white roots tradition, pain and suffering are temporary and will soon be resolved. In the black tradition, pain and suffering are simply part of life. This is a good reminder that people often process similar circumstances quite differently because of the difference in their histories. Human beings eventually come to believe the stories that they tell themselves, and in the West there appears no better teacher than the use of history. I believe part of the reason for racial division lies in the word *division* itself. If *di-* is a prefix meaning "two," and *vision* is the act of seeing, then part of the reason our black/white racial problems continue on stems from the fact that there are two groups of people seeing the same history, the same present, and the same future in two completely different ways.

Hank Williams Sr.

We would probably be on safe footing to give Hank Williams the title of "father of modern country music." Hank Williams's career as a superstar only lasted about four years. This is about the same amount of time that Jimi Hendrix ruled the world of rock music. Eerily, their careers mirrored each other's in one other significant way. Each of them endured the pain of rejection early in their careers only to later cast a wide shadow over their respective genres. It was said of Jimi Hendrix that he changed the face of rock and roll more than any solitary figure in its history. Hank Williams was just as influential for country music. I have heard that there was country music before Hank, and there was country music after Hank. His songs were covered (rerecorded) many times by other artists in the fields of pop, blues, rhythm and blues, and rock. That was unheard of for a country artist at that time. Let us take a minute to look a little closer at one of those covers.

In 1962 Ray Charles, who was both black and blind, recorded an album called *The Modern Sounds in Country and Western Music*. There are two significant facts about this record. First, Ray Charles was an extremely popular rhythm-and-blues artist, and though he was enormously popular among blacks, he bravely recorded songs unfamiliar to his fan base. I was one of those fans. It seems to me that when a person is crossing a dotted line, they do so through any opening that is available to them. I remember being drawn to Ray Charles's version of "Move It On Over," not knowing that it was a song written by a country artist named Hank Williams. For some reason I especially liked the phrase "Move over little dog. / There's a big dog moving in."

Second, *The Modern Sounds in Country and Western Music* was released just as the civil rights movement was gaining momentum. Just think: during the time when racial tensions were escalating in America, the (black) rhythm-and-blues musician Ray Charles decided to record an entire album of nothing but (white) country music. That courageous decision by the physically blind musician displayed uncompromising vision: in Charles's album, two musical styles meshed, which were once viewed as disparate. If musical styles can mesh, then why not races? Genius!

Please remember that country music was generally thought of as the music of the segregated South. This is the region of the country that was ground zero for the oppression of black people. My take on Ray Charles's decision is that he subtly signaled that the past did not matter because the future is yet to be decided. I see that recording as a huge success in two ways. First, black people discovered that they could like and enjoy county music without having to disconnect from their own cultural preferences. And second, whites discovered that they could accept a black person singing their music. This is the type of win-win that we need more of today.

Charlie Pride

I am encouraged by the central fact of the following story. That is that a style of music once the vehicle for dividing groups would one day become the bridge that would begin the process of joining those two groups together. In the past people seemed to gravitate towards certain musical styles only because their group preferred that particular style. I have observed that quite often there is really no other reason than peer pressure for many of the musical choices that people make. My immediate thought is, in how many other facets of life would that be true today? To illustrate this point further, there was a time when this one particular singer was having his songs played on national country radio stations, and they were very popular. The interesting twist in the story is that the primarily white listening audience had no idea that the singer they were enjoying so much was black. His name was Charlie Pride, and he would go on to garner wide acceptance as a genuine country artist.

The Outlaws

Ten to fifteen years after Ray Charles had successfully crossed the color line, creating a new genre in the process, another merger occurred in country music. This time it was not between the music of different racial groups; it was between the rebellious white liberal hippies that loved country and the conservative white country purists. Willie Nelson and his gang of outlaws were the protagonists. The purists viewed them as the equivalent of a group of terrorists bent on destroying the essentials of country. Willie and his cohorts Waylon Jennings, Johnny Cash, Kris Kristofferson, and on occasion Bob Dylan, blurred the line between traditional country music, and the so-called noise produced by the young, suburban, pot-smoking, hippie rock musicians. Hindsight reveals that those musicians did in fact set the world of country music on its heels. The time period between the late 1960s, and the early 1970s was a watershed of cultural change around the world. Country music was not exempt from this change. People were dissatisfied with the way society was structured racially, socioeconomically, and politically, and they were doing something about it. Apparently Willie Nelson and friends were dissatisfied with where country music was at that time, and they did something about it. Gladly, even their harshest critics recognized that the changes that were occurring were actually for the better.

Garth Brooks

Change within country music cannot be discussed without mentioning the name Garth Brooks. Today country music is trying to ward off rap music and television talent contests to keep them from infiltrating country music's fan base. Country-music purists believe that there are clearly established boundary lines in place to keep the "intruders" out of their art. Can you imagine the surprise those purists experienced when they became aware that those once solid lines had already been broken in several places by Garth Brooks! It was not his music per se that rankled the purists, as much as it was his elaborate stage show. Garth's stage presentation was the kind typically reserved for pop icons. Country music had weathered the storm of blacks, hippies, and to a degree rock influences, and now Garth Brooks had brought something possibly more frightening: commercialization!

All the fear surrounding Brooks's emergence may have been totally unnecessary, because at the end of the day Garth may have saved country music rather than killed it. My understanding is that he is the all-time best-selling country-music singer. His popularity opened the door for countless other pop rockers to have success in the country field. There could be a correlation in this for American culture. Many whites in the United States have viewed blacks, hippies, and rockers as people groups that would eventually destroy what it means to be an American. The perception of the evil outsider will always cause people to fear the change that outsiders are bringing with them rather than to embrace it. However, as it relates to music, the reality could be that country music is now bigger and, many would say, better because of the changes that have occurred throughout its history—even though those changes were hardly ever welcomed in real time. Could this be true of our society too? Could country music be a type, a model, for the way our society has reacted to change, and could country music serve to guide a more productive response to societal diversity? Would we be better off to embrace the changes that are certainly coming related to the way our society is structured? Cultural pluralism is upon us, just as musical pluralism penetrated country music. The only pertinent question for us is, how will we respond?

Boundary Lines Become Dotted Lines

Let me close this chapter with an update related to the personal confession that opened this chapter. Hank Williams Jr. is one of the most talented musicians that I have witnessed up close and personal. He helped change my opinion of country music—from my viewing it as too simple to be of much value into a respectful appreciation. Additionally, something happened recently that alerted me to the fact that my prior disdain for the music may have stemmed from my own bigotry towards the people who loved it and those who made it. At the end of the day my opinions about country music may have resulted more from my lack of understanding that anything those involved actually did to me. Remember the concept of similarism? *Similarism* is the word that describes the inclination to automatically assume that life is best lived in the company of people who are similar.

I rejected country music without ever giving it a fair hearing, but thankfully that changed. That change came as a result of me spending time in Jamaica in the 1990s. While there I was surprised to learn that Jamaicans actually like country music. I was surprised that Jamaicans did not know that darker-skinned people were not supposed to like country music. That experience led to the realization that there are several commonalities between country music and reggae. You may be surprised to learn that it does not require much alteration to make a country song into a reggae song, and vice versa. Listen to versions by Toots and the Maytals some of the country songs popular in the 1970s, such as John Denver's "Country Roads," and you will hear what I am talking about. My research for this book led me to see that country music also has some characteristics with other styles as well. It has a lot in common with cajon, zydeco, New Orleans funk, and rock and roll—as well as with blues, and American folk music, as I mentioned earlier. Country music has come a long way from the insular and rigid genre spoken of at the beginning of this chapter. It has become a style of music that is not afraid to cross intergenre borders in search of the new and better. Could it be that the lines that divide musical styles and people are never really as solid as they appear to be—that they are actually dotted lines waiting to be crossed?

10

The Art of Understanding

If you are even marginally familiar with the name Rush Limbaugh, then you may be wondering, what on earth could he possibly have to do with art, understanding, and inclusion? Many would doubt that Rush Limbaugh would be the appropriate celebrity to point to when the topic of inclusion is being discussed. I realize that many see him as one of the more divisive personalities in America. Before I explain why I selected Mr. Limbaugh to illustrate a way to become more inclusive, allow me to make two disclaimers. The first is that I am not much of a fan of the famous radio talk-show host. The second is that I am not inserting his name into our conversation simply to elicit some type of reaction from his admirers or his detractors. I chose Mr. Limbaugh because something happened in his life that changed my perspective on what is needed to improve interpersonal relations. What I am calling the Limbaugh Syndrome is really a template for taking positive steps towards a more open and just society through listening with the intent to understand all that is heard. This is the way that the idea came to me.

Several years ago I was driving my little two-seat sports car by the beach in Boca Raton, Florida. I was enjoying the scent of the ocean breeze and listening to a local news station on the radio when *The Rush Limbaugh Show* began to air. On this particular day Mr. Limbaugh made the decision to discuss some very personal issues. One of those issues was informing his audience that he was practically deaf. I was shocked that a person in his profession could be deaf, even partially deaf, and carry out his radio responsibilities. I also wondered if there was a possibility that he was joking with his listeners for some reason. I considered changing the station to music, but curiosity got the better of me. He continued on to say that he was severely deaf and that he had just had a device called a cochlear implant installed in his ear. The cochlea is the part of the middle ear that receives and then amplifies sound vibrations. The way the implant works is similar to the way my bass amplifier magnifies a note being played on my electric guitar. My electric bass will not make a sound that is audible to an audience unless it is amplified. In essence, Rush had a variation of a bass amplifier implanted in his ear. Therefore, words spoken would not be audible to him without the implant. That day he was informing his listeners that the device just marginally improved his hearing, that it would not be a fix, but that he was thankful for the device and optimistic about the future.

What is relevant to our discussion is the way that Limbaugh's hearing was improved by the use of the implant. He said that even though the device did amplify the sounds around him, he still had difficulty understanding the words being spoken to him. He could hear them, but he could not understand them. He said that when people spoke to him, they sounded "fuzzy." Listening to him describe his hearing difficulty caused me to think that his medical condition could be analogous to how human beings interact with each other. Often times we are aware of the words that people are saying around us, but we do not always understand them or their intended meaning. If this is true, then it follows that developing the skill to understand better could be a valuable tool for repairing division. One prerequisite to understanding is to become aware of the filters that we unintentionally develop throughout life.

Many times we hear a certain type of music and dislike it on first hearing. Quite often we reject that music simply because we are not familiar with it, and so we do not understand it. I remember one occurrence when I had purchased a new CD, by guitarist Greg Howe and bassist Victor Wooten called *Extraction*. I was very excited about this particular CD because these two musicians are masters in their fields. I was eager to share my find with a colleague named Patsy Frantanduono because I knew that she liked both jazz and bass. She borrowed the disc, kept it for a couple weeks, and then returned it without comment. That prompted me to ask how she liked it, and she responded, "It was a little too esoteric for me."

Actually, her facial expression implied that she really did not care for the music all that much. I made a mental note of how politely she rejected "my" music and let the matter rest. However, I did learn a valuable lesson in the process. Patsy and I were both pastors at Cedar Ridge Community Church and great friends. We were also huge fans of the great bassist Stanley Clarke. However, our similarities ended there. I was at one time a professional bassist, and she, while a lover of music, had never been a performer of music. I would speculate that one reason Patsy did not share my enthusiasm for *Extraction* is that the music on that CD is very technical, and this made it difficult for nonmusicians to understand. Quite often it is not so much a matter of unfamiliarity that prevents a person from appreciating a different style of music. Rather, it is a lack of understanding of what is being played that is the problem. In a similar way, a lack of understanding can keep us from appreciating how people from different faith traditions practice their faith.

I am co-chair of the Interfaith Arts Council, which stages music events to allow people from different faith traditions to come together to enjoy sacred music and cultural exchange. I am also involved with the Austin Interfaith Inclusion Network. What we do is help local congregations of all faiths include more people living with disabilities. Interfaith work is challenging because the people involved must set aside their fear and mistrust of the other. Here is an example of the way problems can surface when people do not make the effort to understand those they see as the other. A rabbi friend brought a choir from her synagogue to sing at an ecumenical function at a Baptist church. The plan was for both choirs to sing together at some point during the program. The music director at the Baptist-church choir selected a few songs for them to sing that contained references to Jesus. The rabbi thought it a bit odd that the leadership of the church would not be more sensitive to her tradition. Jewish congregations do not sing songs to or about Jesus. On the other hand, I am sure that the Baptist leadership simply assumed that most people would expect there to be some singing about Jesus in a Baptist church.

Let us scratch beneath the surface of that misunderstanding. First, most Jewish people rarely attend Christian church services, and so why should they be aware of what may or may not happen inside of one? Second, the members of the synagogue choir were the guests at the Baptist church. One could argue that it is the host's responsibility to make sure that the guests feel comfortable. I should insert one personal observation here as a Christian minister: Most of my colleagues rarely attend the services of other faiths. They are not aware that there are many faith traditions outside

Christianity that do not ever sing songs to their deities. Perhaps my colleagues assume that other faith traditions do some variation of liturgy similar to theirs. Can you see why assumptions can quite often be the mortal enemy of understanding? Too many times we never get past the assumption stage when we are interacting with people we believe to be different. Most interfaith conflict really does come from a lack of understanding about the basic teaching of another's faith. This misunderstanding of another's faith results in a misunderstanding of an adherent's intentions, and we have a difficult time understanding why adherents of that other faith community do what they do.

The Baptist minister could certainly argue, "Should it be an issue for me to ask a Jewish person to sing a couple songs that have Jesus' name mentioned in the lyrics?"

I am sure that some Christians would think, That is right! After all, Jesus was Jewish, and so what could be the harm?

The rabbi, on the other hand, knows that many in her congregation view Jesus not so much as a religious figure, but as a symbol of injustice perpetrated on the Jewish people in his name. In a sense the tension is not so much about the Jesus of the Bible as it is about what has been done in his name at certain times in history.

This example illustrates how important proper understanding is, and it also underscores how problems arise when it is absent. The average evangelical today has little knowledge about the history of their tradition. For this reason it is very hard for some evangelicals to understand why some people outside the tradition see them as something other than a group of loving people, which most are by the way.

Let us examine our illustration a little more closely. We have just discussed a situation where a small amount of tension surfaced between two religious organizations due to a misunderstanding. Think about who these people are: They are both spiritually based groups, and they would both be classified as racially majority-white groups. Both are American, and both share the same book as the foundation of their faith. However, none of those similarities immunized the Baptists, in this case, from showing insensitivity to their Jewish guests.

Why have humans beings behaved insensitively throughout our history? Why do we seem to focus on differences before we are willing to even look at the things we hold in common? What if the Christian faith was simply about authentically loving God, and sincerely loving our neighbor?

What if faith is not so much about majoring in a particular set of abstract ideas and behaviors? Then the important questions might be, what is God like, and who is our neighbor? Instead of asking these questions, we focus on an attender's beliefs about baptism and worship style, on the demographics of the attenders, and on so many ancillary things that there is always a door for conflict to enter.

Happy Together?

I mentioned earlier that I am on the board of a nonprofit named the Interfaith Arts Council (IAC). A friend recently asked how I could be so deeply involved in projects with clergy who do not believe as I believed. I thought about the question for several months before realizing that the answer was found in the question itself. My friend's concern was that my beliefs about God could be compromised by the beliefs of the clergy of different faith traditions on the board. My friend's question may have been rooted in the wrong concern. Perhaps before engaging me with this question, my friend should have considered the following question, should what Jimi's colleagues on the IAC board believe be more important to him than what kind of people they are? Had I even remotely believed that my friend had thought his question through before he inquired about our organization, I would have asked him a question in return. I would have asked, what does our tradition teach about how we are to view a person, any person? Then in true Socratic form I would have said, once you have answered what you believe constitutes a person, then I will explain why I collaborate with persons from different faith traditions. The Christian tradition teaches that a human being is more than the sum total of an occupation, a physical appearance, a skin color, and even of religious views held at any given time. This suggests that it may not be wise for any of us to judge someone on any one—or all—of these characteristics.

Have you noticed that the world has become a much smaller place? Businesspeople now run transcontinental corporations, and we call that *globalization*. People are on the move too. Every major city in the U.S. now has some type of a minority immigrant community within its borders. Such an immigrant community is more than the food, language, and social customs that the community brings to this country. They bring their religion too. How will we respond? How should we respond? If you are a Christian, then you are likely aware that we Christians have a long history of arguing with one another about correct beliefs about God. A focus on correct beliefs leads to the assumption that the more knowledge a person has about spiritual things, the more spiritually mature a person is. Such an assumption eventually leads to our comparing our knowledge with the knowledge of others. Then we proceed to debate (fight) in order to win the battle over who holds the superior knowledge concerning an issue of theology.

In Christian circles the religious beliefs that churches teach are called *doctrines*. Teaching good doctrine is important for the nurture of the soul and the propagation of the faith. But notice that I said *good*, instead of *right* or *correct*. In my view, good doctrine feeds the spirit and the soul, and it is the spirit that draws one closer to God. The fact that the spirit is involved suggests that the acquisition of knowledge for knowledge's sake does not make anyone more spiritual. A saying in evangelical circles goes like this: "Attending church will not make you a Christian any more than sitting in a garage will make you a car." In keeping with the logic, if books made people spiritual, then libraries and not churches would be the places to find God. The end result of gaining knowledge in a Christian should be for the acquisition of tools that will help a person love more rather than know more.

This is important when dealing with people whom you view as different. They have knowledge too. Additionally, they may believe that their knowledge is equal to yours, and that could actually be true. So if your interaction with people different from you includes judging them by what they know or believe, what happens next? Engage in a debate each time you are together? Avoid any contact with the person in order to be spared from having to hear their strange views? No. I suggest that you extend the equal amount of grace to them that you have received. You could be wondering, how would that look? How about this? If they are right, you love them; if they are wrong, you love them even more. My understanding is that spiritual maturity points a person towards the direction of humility when it comes to knowledge. This view contrasts starkly with the "knowledge-is-power" position from academia. Knowledge of God is not power but love.

I would like to now draw an analogy from another art form, martial arts, to illustrate the importance of keeping the main thing the main thing. My friend and my former Kung Fu *sifu* is named Dane Junod. A student once asked him how to defend against multiple attackers. Without hesitation, he smiled and said, "Run!" Now please understand that his comment was half in jest, but it does make a point. The goal of martial-arts training is survival and not winning fights. Similarly, the goal of spiritual knowledge is to be more loving and understanding, and not to arm oneself with tools to win arguments. When a martial artist walks away from a fight that could probably be won, the choice of a peaceful resolution is made from a position of strength, not weakness. Similarly, when we choose not to engage in spiritual arguments with people, and to love them as they are, we are also operating from a position of strength and not weakness.

Why am I able to make that assertion with such confidence? Did not Jesus have all power in the universe at his disposal and choose not to use it? Loving the outsider should not be a strategy to convert people to your faith. Loving people should not only be a church slogan or a position statement on a webpage. In martial arts a stance (for instance, a horse stance) is part of a fighting posture that gives the practitioner stability. In many instances a fighter's stance is so stable that an adversary cannot force the one in this stance to move. In sum, the best stance a Christian can assume imitates the open arms of Christ on the cross. This stance will broadcast to others that the person is willing to assume a posture of sacrifice and welcome for the good of the other, even when the other is a stranger. Many in the West are terrified at the prospect that a pluralistic society is not only close at hand but inevitable. Those who fear pluralism would like for Western hegemony to last forever. I am learning through my interfaith relationships that I can remain in my stance on doctrinal positions while treating the stranger with value and dignity by emulating the posture of love modeled by Christ.

During this era of rapidly changing demographics it is important that every person accept responsibility to see the stranger as a unique work of art created by God. Human beings share common DNA before they are individually an accountant, a Hindu, a person with disabilities, a Bangladeshi, or whatever. Because of this, people who identify with the Christian faith should strive to treat each individual living on the planet like the family member that they truly are, and then love them.

I came across a very interesting article in the popular magazine called *Christianity Today*. The article contained statistics that should give pause to those who practice the Christian tradition and believe that the idea of welcome is part of their faith's heritage. Missiologist Todd M. Johnson and his team found that "20 percent of non-Christians in North America do not 'personally know' any Christians. That's 13,447,000 people—about the population of metropolitan Los Angeles or Istanbul—most of them in the United States"[1] After considering the ramifications of those percentages, the question should be, why do those statistics exist? What is it that we are doing, or not doing, that signals to the outsider that they are not welcome?

The article goes on to quote the missiologist Johnson as saying that the major reason for the high number of people not knowing any Christians is immigration. Most of us are aware that immigration has been a political hot-button topic in America for years. My view is that we spend a considerable amount of time discussing if or when people should be allowed to settle here in the U.S. However, we spend very little time discussing what will happen when they do arrive. Many of you have seen images that depict what the world would look like (in terms of population percentages) if there were only one hundred people in it. If you have not seen one, here is a sampling of the numbers of one of the many available. It says that 61 percent of people would be Asian, 13 percent would be African, 13 percent would be located in the Americas, and 12 percent would be European. Finally, 1 percent would be Oceanian.[2] People of European descent rarely view themselves as a global minority group, and so they rarely consider what the implications of that might be. But the world is getting smaller, and the U.S. is changing. Perhaps now is time to consider what our attitudes should be regarding outsiders and strangers.

I was once an immigrant to the Central American country of Belize. I resided in that little slice of heaven for a little over eight years. I know first hand what it feels like to not know the verbal and nonverbal signals that people in an unfamiliar environment use. What I mean by "signals" are things like jokes, body language, adages, myths, legends, and commonly accepted folklore. No matter how hard I tried to fit in, there was always some sort of invisible fence separating me from automatic acceptance.

Conversely, we in the U.S. often send signals to immigrants that they are not fully accepted. For some reason it seems to be an automatic human reflex to fear the stranger rather than make the effort to understand the stranger. We see the immigrant in many different ways, but rarely do we see them as an artist's rendering from the fingertips of God. Missiologist Todd Johnson thinks that "America is suffering from a serious deficit of

---

1. Stocker, "Craziest Statistic," sections 2 and 3.

2. http://webodysseum.com/various/if-the-world-were-100-people-what-would-it-look-like/ (fourth image down).

hospitality."[3] This could very well be true, but I am confident that we can and will do better once we develop an understanding ear.

Topography and Soundscapes

Topography is a term that describes the arrangement of the physical features and characteristics present in a particular environment. The mountains that overlook the Pacific Ocean are part of the topography of western Los Angeles County in California. There are also hotels, surf shops, and houses close to the beach in that same area. They are also part of the topography. Those items that I just listed could also be referred to as part of the landscape. My adopted hometown is Manhattan Beach, California. It is a beach city whose streets slope down some subtle rolling hills to a gorgeous beach. Were I to describe the landscape to someone, I would include the hilltop vistas, the muscled surfers and volleyball players enjoying their sun-blessed activities, and the beautiful sunbathers who checker the sandy beaches as well. This would mean that in the way I'm using it, the term *topography* is applicable to a city, state, or country and includes people and things in addition to the natural terrain. Simply put, my definition of *topography* consists of all of the elements located on top of a specific geography.

The topography, or the landscape, of any given area is usually in a state of flux. Let me illustrate with a story from my music career. Several years ago I was touring the state of California with an English jazz musician named Brian Auger. One of the cities where we were scheduled to perform was Santa Cruz. I had lived in Santa Cruz ten years before this tour, and I was excited about coming home. Leading up to our performance date I spent a considerable amount of time telling my band mates what a wonderful time we would have in Santa Cruz. I prepped them about what to do and where to go to have a good time. As we drove down from San Francisco, which was about an hour-and-a-half drive, I continued to sing the praises of this quaint little beach town. However, once we entered the city I found that the topography had changed to the extent that I recognized very little. Santa Cruz had grown significantly which meant that there were many new roads and buildings that were unfamiliar to me. I was soon to be embarrassed even further because after several attempts to locate the venue where we were to play, I had to stop and get directions. I could feel doubting eyes from the back of the van saying, "Sure, you used to live here."

3. Ibid., section 14.

Santa Cruz is not the only place whose topography has changed. Our country's topography is changing, and changing rapidly. The overall landscape may not be changing that fast, but the infrastructure of our cities is changing. The ethnicities of the people living in our cities are changing as well. For many people change is unsettling if not flat-out frightening. When that change has a perceived effect on any one particular group's economic status it becomes an even more frightening proposition. But should fear be the appropriate reaction to the stranger, or should it be welcome? Perhaps music can assist us in finding the answer to the last question. I am also suggesting that music can offer some solutions too.

Soundscapes

I would like to introduce a new word into our discussion, and the word is *soundscape*. *Soundscape* is a term used to describe "the component of sounds of an environment, and the component sounds of a piece of music."[4] I am suggesting that a soundscape is to music what topography is to geography. Topography describes how the physical characteristics of a particular geography are arranged. In a similar way the word *soundscape* describes the way created sounds are arranged. To illustrate, think about the number of sounds that can exist within any given environment. Now consider the way that those sounds relate to each other.

Imagine walking down a busy street in downtown New York City. The street is in the process of being repaired, and the sounds made by the jackhammers and other construction equipment are loud and constant. This causes the noonday traffic to move at a snails pace. Impatient New Yorkers are laying on the horns of their automobiles because they are anxious to satisfy their hunger pains. While this is happening you can hear noises coming from passing planes. An emergency vehicle's siren is blasting from a neighboring street. How these environmental sounds are arranged within your psyche is analogous to how sounds are arranged within a musical soundscape. The word *soundscape* not only addresses what sounds are being heard by a person; the word also speaks to the *way* those sounds are heard, as well as the effect they have on the listener.

Let us now focus on musical soundscapes. The synthesizer is an electronic-keyboard instrument popularized in the 1970s. It operates pretty

4. Dictionary.com/, s.v. "Soundscape," http://dictionary.reference.com/browse/sound scape/.

much the same way a computer operates. It has an internal memory, so the synthesizer can produce computerized sounds from other keyboard instruments such as an organ and a piano A synthesizer can also produce sounds that mimic other instruments such as guitars, trumpets, saxophones, drums, violins, and so forth. Are you aware of how much computer technology has advanced in the last twenty years? Twenty years ago I moved to Belize with an Apple computer called an SE-30. I presently own an Apple MacBook Pro. My MacBook Pro is 330 times more powerful than my SE-30 was. Synthesizers have followed a similar improvement track in terms of processing power. The result is that the average listener can date music from different eras if electronic keyboards were utilized in the music. This is because new synthesizer sounds are being created almost daily. Manufacturers are continually tweaking the timbre, or color, of the synthesized sounds of their products. For this reason you can actually hear a perceptible difference between keyboards from one era to the next.

What that should say to us is that music seems to allow for innovation, change, and improvement within its soundscapes. In fact, the majority of musicians I know actually welcome most of the changes as they materialize. Many times musicians are not only pursuing change; they are causing it. Our society would do well to adopt a musician's attitude when it comes to welcoming the outsider. Musicians embrace change, but far too often our society fears it. A musician who does not respond to the changing tastes of the audience becomes antiquated and left behind. Perhaps we should remember that the old way is not always good enough when it comes to the soundscape of interpersonal relations

Blinded by Sight

Did you know that many people often decide whether or not they like a certain musician by the visual impression the performer makes on them, rather than by the performer's musical skill? My friend Bryan Anderson recently sent me an article about a young musician named Chia-Jung Tsay. The article related Chia's experiences of not having her music accepted for what it was:

> She was something of a piano prodigy and at 16 she made her debut at Carnegie Hall. Soon, she was on her way to some of the best music schools in the country—Juilliard, and the Peabody Conservatory. Getting into the schools and competitions often

required auditions, and different auditions had different rules. Some required audio recordings. Others required video. The judges all said they were evaluating her music, but Tsay started to notice a pattern.[5]

Tsay said, "I noticed that for whatever reason I seemed to be doing better when I submitted video recordings, or when the auditions or competitions involved live-rounds kinds of evaluations,"[6] It appears that her results were much better when people could *see* and hear the music as compared to when they could only hear it.

Very early in this book I put forward the idea that visual art has always had a profound effect on the culture around it. In our highly mediated world there may be no better example of how much we depend on visuals than the way we get our news. Most of us get our news from the newspaper, television, or computer. These forms of media deliver their information visually. In the last few years the news media have covered several high-profile shootings. In Newtown Connecticut, a twenty-year-old white male shot and killed twenty unsuspecting children. A few years before that incident, two white teenagers shot and killed fifteen students at Columbine High School in Colorado. As I write this, three black teenagers are charged with killing an Australian baseball player. The media are reporting that they committed the crime for the "fun of it," or "because they were bored."[7] At this writing, another pending court case making headlines involves two black teenagers who are alleged to have killed a white baby in a stroller somewhere in Georgia.[8]

While the brutality of these senseless killings has no direct bearing on our conversation, the way that the media chooses to report them does. The majority of news outlets that I have watched have represented the white offenders at Columbine and Newtown to be youths who were acting of out the norm because they were "troubled." However, the black offenders were referred to as "thugs" by many commentators; these commentators imply that their involvement in criminal behavior was characteristic of them rather than anomalous.

Implicit in this representation is that one people group (whites) is innately more moral than another (blacks). Common sense would then

5. Vedantam, "How to Win That Music Competition? Send a Video."

6. Ibid.

7. Carreras, "Christopher Lane."

8. Watkins et al., "Baby Shot Dead in Stroller."

dictate that the (white) moral people group should be in charge of shaping and controlling our society. Once this perception is firmly embedded in the minds of the majority, an unjust social order soon follows. We must learn to see every created being as the art of God, and not only to see people from our group as having value. Then when an individual deviates from their created purpose by committing a crime, we will simply call the person a criminal, without assigning any other meanings to the word *criminal.*

> "It is only with the heart that one can see rightly; what is essentially invisible to the eye."
>
> —Antoine de Saint-Exupery

One other thing that my interfaith efforts have taught me is that there are principles in each religion that are common to all. Often those familiar principles can appear to be very different from Christian teaching because they are couched in the vocabulary of another faith. They can also sound like different principles when they are coming from the lips of a person who looks different from you. When I was a younger pastor, I perceived that it was almost a sin to admit commonalities between religions. I thought to do so would be giving some sort of tactical advantage to a competing religion. Let us look at the principle of mutual reciprocity that we often call the Golden Rule. Let us look at two other faith traditions that have a similar idea as part of their teaching on social ethics. Muhammad said, "None of you have faith unless you desire for your neighbor what you desire for yourself."[9] The Jewish sage Hillel said, "That which is hateful to you, do not do to your fellow."[10] Jesus said in Mark chapter 12, "Love your neighbor as yourself."[11] It is worth remembering that he said that there is no greater commandment than this one and the injunction to love God. Just think, these identical spiritual principles are found in religions presently experiencing tension politically. For some reason we instinctively allow perceived difference to trump similarities in a way that will cause us to do the opposite of what our faiths command us to do. That certainly needs to change!

9. Volf, *Allah,* 29.

10. Beck, *God of One's Own,* 159.

11. Mark 12:31.

Understanding a piece of music begins with listening. Listening is an acquired skill. Understanding people different from you begins with listening. Listening to people is also an acquired skill. Mr. Limbaugh voiced frustration at having to relearn how to listen that day on the radio. He heard sounds, but he had to develop the concentration necessary to transpose those sounds into words. Limbaugh also had to develop the skill to understand the words being spoken as he was hearing them. His radio program is of the listener-call-in variety. This means that the listening audience calls the program in order to talk with the host, Rush Limbaugh, about a wide range of topics and news items. Can you imagine the problems that would occur on his radio program if he assumed that he understood what the callers were saying when he actually did not! Mr. Limbaugh knew that his condition meant that he had the responsibility to do what was necessary to understand his callers by listening intently. He was willing to make the effort, and his effort paid off in the form of continued popularity in spite of his hearing problems.

I am an African American male who has spent most of my career working in churches where the majority of attenders were white. Any success that I have achieved professionally has come as a direct result of my making the effort to understand the perspectives and values of the white attenders. Should it ever become the desire of a large number of white people to understand black people, I suggest that these white people try to listen more to what is being said, instead of the way it is being said. Far too many conversations between black and white people have stalled simply because of differences in vocabulary. I can recall conversations in which both white and black people genuinely seek to understand the other, all are earnestly trying to listen, but word choices by the other party prevent each party from understanding the other.

Let us sit in on a conversation that a Native American elder named Dan had with an inquisitive white visitor he calls Nerburn in a book titled *Neither Wolf nor Dog*. The conversation between Dan and Nerburn illustrates just how easy it is for any of us to misunderstand the intentions of the other. Dan said this in response to a question about the way indigenous people see the "settling" of America: "You need to understand this. We did not think we owned the land. The land was part of us. We didn't even know about owning land. It is like talking about owning your grandmother. You can't own your grandmother. She is just your grandmother."[12]

12. Nerburn, *Neither Wolf nor Dog*, 46.

Here Dan, the Native American elder, is not just commenting on one particular incident or conversation. He is contrasting two fundamentally different understandings of land usage. He has just articulated the native population's understanding about their land, and then he points out why there was a misunderstanding between his people and white settlers.

Yet Dan's conversation partners missed the meaning behind the words he used. Dan went on to say, "Your people did not know about the land being sacred. We did not know about the land being property. We could not talk because we did not understand each other."[13] Communication is only valuable when it leads to understanding. I believe that were we to put forth the time and energy necessary to really understand the other—more than simply hearing the words of the other—that good would automatically follow. Then we would no longer struggle building bridges between each other because the art of understanding would provide a direct flight.

13. Ibid., 49.

11

Roots and Culture

Jazz, blues, and country are three musical styles rooted and cultivated in the musical soundscape we call Americana, music indigenous to North America. Another name for that style of music is *roots music*. Every geographic region and every culture has its own distinctive style of music that would qualify as its roots music. The style called Americana also contains ingredients derived from a European base that is primarily Irish and Scottish in origin. The music of Asia, Africa, and to a lesser degree the southern portion of the Americas, is often rooted in non-European forms. The musicians living in each region have a completely different way of organizing their music, and that results in much of their music sounding quite different from ours. This is because music, like culture, is most often a derivation of the worldview of the people who established the roots of that specific society. Roots and culture are inseparable. Asian, African, and South American music can also sound different from European and North American music because some instruments from Asia, Africa, and South America use different tunings than do instruments common in Europe and North America. The tuning difference can result in the use of different scales for writing songs. The tunings alone can cause non-Western music to sound almost dissonant to the Western ear. It requires a serious amount of effort by Western people to remember that the different sounds present in non-Western music does not make it inferior to Western music.

In the middle of the last century Western musicians began to take an interest in the music of India. The Beatles became interested in Indian spirituality, and that led them to the music of the great sitarist Ravi Shankar. Notice that art and spirituality are often times natural partners. I see the two as interdisciplinary activities rather than separate activities. For example, many believe that the music that attracted the attention of the Beatles was derived from the Indian scriptures called Vedas. It is commonly assumed that even the scales used in Indian music originated in the chants offered in various temples throughout India. Indian music has a linear and melodic style, in contrast with the chordal and harmonic style foundational to the jazz, blues, and country styles enjoyed in the West. For this reason Indian music can be difficult for us Westerners to understand and appreciate, but it is a wonderful, even beautiful, art form.

The great jazz saxophonist John Coltrane became interested in Indian music at about the same time as the Beatles. Just as the Beatles interest did, so Coltrane's interest stemmed from his admiration for Ravi Shankar. Mr. Coltrane appeared to be so enamored with the virtuoso sitarist that Coltrane named his son Ravi Coltrane. John Coltrane was also interested in African scales and rhythms. At one point his music became very controversial because he decided to incorporate the styles of Asia and Africa into his music. Today there is an entire CD dedicated to that exploratory period of Mr. Coltrane's career when he sought to blend Eastern musical roots and culture with that of the West. The CD, performed and produced by percussionist Anthony Brown, is aptly named *India & Africa: A Tribute to John Coltrane.*[1]

John Coltrane felt it necessary to embrace and absorb another culture's approach to music in order to broaden his scope both musically and spiritually. Coltrane's musical quest in search of what he perceived would be good for his growth could provide a model for the way we do race, religion, and ethics within our culture. We could learn from him that it is acceptable—possibly even desirable—to welcome those we perceive to be different from us, then absorb aspects of their culture that are beneficial while retaining and maintaining our own. For Coltrane, the incorporation of styles outside his own was (so to speak) a win-win, and I suppose the same would hold true were we to become more receptive of those with different cultural backgrounds. From reading one of his biographies I sense that Mr. Coltrane saw creating better music as only part of the benefit he

---

1. Brown and His Asian American Orchestra, *India & Africa.*

would receive once he inserted himself into another culture. He traveled to Africa because he understood that blending musical soundscapes—even ones that Westerners considered so different that they should not be inte-grated—could be done successfully. Coltrane's music did prove that friction is not always the end result of blending musical roots and culture, regard-less of how different the musical roots and cultures appear on the surface.

Blending Soundscapes

This chapter began with our discussing the blending of soundscapes at a macrolevel. John Coltrane and the Beatles blended complete musical styles into their own while absorbing some of the culture that produced the style. I would now like to discuss the way musical soundscapes are blended at the microlevel (at the level of the music we purchase as consumers). My experience in the record industry exposed me to the reality that there is more to creating a great record than simply identifying cool songs, recruit-ing good musicians to play them, and then recording them. The majority of music offered in the commercial marketplace undergoes a process called "the mix" prior to being released. Mixing a record is the process that takes all of the voices and instruments that were recorded, and then blends them in such a fashion that all of the parts are in balance. The mixing process is vital for the creation of music that is both good art and a viable commercial product.

The mixing process does not receive a lot of recognition, but it can be as important as the actual musical performance by the artist. Many great pieces of music have been ruined when the mix was substandard. Artists can put together all the right ingredients necessary for success, only to have a failure on their hands when the various elements were not blended properly. Can you imagine listening to a record where the voices and in-struments were not positioned properly? Imagine hearing a track on the radio where the singer was considerably louder than the instruments! What about the guitar drowning out everything else in the background? The goal of the mix engineer is to position the voices and instruments in such a way that they are complementary, with the hope that the music will be pleasing to the ear.

Before we discuss this one specific type of blending, I would like to in-troduce one last musical term: *timbre*. In prior chapters we have discussed pitch, rhythm, chords, harmony—and now it is time that we look at a word that influences the way we process the music that we hear. *Timbre* is the word used to describe both the characteristics of the tone and the coloring of the musical sound. When I say that timbre is both tone and color, you may think that I am still speaking about the sound that a particular note makes. In a sense you would be correct because timbre is a part of "the sound" that causes a note to be music. However, timbre does occupy its own niche within the overall musical soundscape.

To illustrate why timbre is a completely different element from simply a musical sound, please try this simple exercise. Relax and close your eyes for a few moments. Now visualize a symphony orchestra playing a piece by one of the classical composers discussed earlier. Imagine what a violin sounds like. Now try to imagine what a trumpet sounds like. Okay, now imagine that they are both playing the note C, and they are playing the note at the same pitch and volume. Would they sound the same in your imagination? No, of course not. The reality is that they would not even sound similar, and the reason is that each instrument produces a distinguishable timbre.

When mixing a record it is not enough to decide which parts you want to have featured, or how the sound of the instruments will fit together. The engineer must also consider whether or not the timbre of each instrument will blend. Each individual instrument not only produces its own unique sound and tone. Each instrument also produces its own shade or tonal color. You have probably witnessed a marching band with a person carrying a large coned horn that resembles a snake wrapped around the player's neck. The instrument is a sousaphone, and it produces many of the same notes as an electric bass guitar. The difference in the timbre of the notes that a sousaphone produces is a sound that will affect you in a completely different way than will the sound produced by an electric bass. This is true even if the sousaphone and the bass were to play the same notes.

Can you see a parallel between the electric bass and sousaphone comparison and the way we often perceive racial difference? Would you perceive that a black person practicing law would produce a different "vocational timbre" than a white person practicing law? In a theoretical sense, the majority of people would most likely answer that question no. However, in everyday practice we seem to arrive at the opposite conclusion. Instead of seeking to blend human instruments together, many today are reverting to the mindset that white doctors would be more effective caring for white patients than black or Asian doctors would be; that black teachers would do a better job teaching urban youth than a Native American teacher would; and so forth.

Allow me to illustrate why this type of thinking is not only antiquated but could be counterproductive to mixing the masterpieces called human beings. Put on a set of imaginary glasses, and envision what an orchestra of fifteen electric basses would look and sound like. How about thirty trombones? The combinations of instruments just mentioned could execute a piece of music to perfection, but they would not sound the way an orchestra typically does, would they? Homogeneity is the norm in our business culture, and also in our church culture. But as I just illustrated, homogeneity makes for a very monotonous musical and cultural product. Making "music" with only those instruments, or people groups, that are the same will probably not sound like an orchestra should to the ear of the person who matters most, God.

To illustrate further, what would you imagine the result would be if we attempted to blend Scottish bagpipes, a couple of Indian sitars, together with a few trombones to record a country-music CD? My guess is that we would definitely have a problem with the traditional country-music aficionadoes, because they would never accept the sound of the music made by this group of instruments as legitimate country music. Sure, those instruments are capable of playing the notes correctly, but their distinctive timbres will prevent the music from sounding genuinely country.

Similarly, were we to blend an African research scholar, a white farmer from Iowa, and a stand-up comic from the Philippines together in order to create racial reconciliation, we would need to be sensitive to the difference in the idiosyncratic timbre or aspect of each occupation prior to devising the best strategy for mixing them. You see a good mix engineer must not only blend parts, voices, and tones. She must also place them in such positions that each element—whether instrument or people group—sounds *its* best. Blending the many disparate sounds into one in order to achieve a better whole *is* the goal of a mix. That should be our goal for the blending the disparate sounds that we call races too. A better whole happens to be the same goal that people have when they become involved in choral singing. Let us see what we can learn from that grouping of people.

Choirs

The possibility of people living harmoniously for a common good cannot ever be realized until we find a way to overcome one formidable foe: individualism. Stacy Horn has written a book titled *Imperfect Harmony: Finding Happiness Singing with Others*. The basic premise of this book is that there are many benefits attached to singing in a choir. One benefit is the sense of accomplishment that the vocalists feel at the performance. Social and psychological benefits also come with working with others to achieve something that could not be achieved individually. Horn implies that the thread that weaves everything together, and what makes choral singing so beneficial, is the joy of accomplishing something *together*. Her book relates several personal life lessons learned from her association with the Choral Society of Grace Church in New York City.

Reading Ms. Horn's wonderful book brought to my mind a few personal life lessons that I learned from choral singing as a youth. These lessons came not from my direct involvement in a choir but through my observations of the dynamics of my church's choir. When I was growing up, my mother was the choir director at our little church named Antioch Baptist Church. Many nights I was required to accompany her to rehearsals. I did not like missing my favorite television shows, and I did not like the music all that much either. However, I did enjoy watching the way the choir members behaved each week. The minidramas that unfolded at each Thursday night rehearsal replaced the television dramas that I was missing. One fundamental rule for successful choral singing is that each person must pay attention when another section is rehearsing a part. My mom had a friend in the choir named Roberta Tee. She had a very hard time with that concept. Frankly, she just loved to talk. It appeared that anytime there was a lull in the action, Mrs. Tee interpreted it as a cue to strike up a conversation with someone around her. All things do work together for good though. I did get to see a gentler side of my mom through this, and I learned that it is possible to positively interact with a person with whom you are not overly pleased, and to do so in a patient, gentle, and loving manner.

Another insight that I picked up on those Thursday nights was that the choir director needed to be aware of everything that was going on, and to be sensitive to the needs of every member. That sensitivity needed to be extended to each member of the choir regardless of what skill they possessed, or what their status was within the choir. A local church choir comes into being through the efforts of volunteers. For that reason my mom made it a priority not to treat the choir members like employees, or subordinates, but like peers. She also wanted to see them succeed within the group context, while she also desired the best for each of them individually. The choir members were a diverse lot. Apart from being Baptist, they really did not have much in common. Yet, for those two hours on every choir-rehearsal night, they were together doing their absolute best to operate as one. How refreshing that one-for-all attitude is when contrasted with the typical self-focused attitude that prevails in much of our culture today! This would signal that there is hope that people can subordinate the desire to please the self to a desire for the good of the many. At its core, the gospel is not only reconciling God with humanity, but also reconciling all of humanity—humans with one another. Perhaps in a demonstrative sense there may be no greater example of blending the many into one than singing in a choir.

Stacy Horn says the following about singing in a choir: "If singing in a choir has taught me anything, it's that what may initially seem strange and dissonant can later strike the most harmonious chords in your life."[2] Race relations in America have begun so horribly, but this does not mean that they cannot end harmoniously. That can happen if all races learn to function more like a choir and less like competing gangs. Just think: within a small choir of maybe a hundred people there are louder voices, and there are softer voices. There are voices that hold their pitch better than others, and there are also members who process rhythms differently. It can be quite a challenge for the director to get them all to sing the same thing, at the exact same time, and in the same way. What should bring us hope is that, challenges aside, it does actually happen!

Gangs

There appears to be a return to the tribalism of our agrarian forebears in many American cities. The old fissures of the Jim Crow 1950s are gradually returning. Today more people are becoming comfortable stating in many public forums that they believe in legally separating races. I recently read an online op-ed piece from a major newspaper suggesting that a return to legal segregation would ease the current rise in racial tension. Yes, even

2. Horn, *Imperfect Harmony*, 25.

today the "separate-but-equal" idea left over from the Jim Crow era sounds appealing to some people. The fact that the newspaper printed the article suggests there may be more people sympathetic to the idea than would admit it. The phrase *racial group* is really nothing more than another way of saying "tribe." Let us imagine that *tribe* is another way of saying "gang." Would you agree that if I used the word *gang* to describe a group separated by race, the idea of separation by race suddenly sounds less attractive? Just imagine the morning news: "The brown-skinned gang of parents met with the lighter-skinned gang of parents at the local middle school to discuss ways to improve grades." Appealing? I think not.

However, this is exactly what we do when we preface what we say about a person by identifying the person's physical features. What we are really doing is identifying the person's tribal or gang affiliation by their "colors"—in this instance, by skin color. That is the same process used when crimes are reported in the media today. Race is frequently the lens through which we are asked to interpret a crime story. The result of this continued bombardment of racial images in the media is that we seem to be drifting farther apart from each other, instead of blending. In fact, even though the legalized apartheid of the recent past is no more, we continue to volitionally isolate ourselves from each other. Self-segregation along racial lines in our churches and in our neighborhoods does exist, and it is pervasive. We like to refer to present-day culture as being postracial, but when it gets down to what really matters, such as where people live and worship, our preferences indicate that we may be as divided as we have ever been. Separation by racial preference or because of racial animus is still separation.

It may not be a stretch to say that we are comfortable viewing other human beings more like rival gang members than as relatives by DNA. Rival gangs view blending with other gangs as something to be avoided at any cost, and it is something that no gang will hardly ever do voluntarily. I certainly hope that this is not the direction that most of us really want to go in regards to race. Let us hope that this tendency is just a bad habit left over from times gone by. As I have already stated, the media are really not helping us to break those bad habits either. This is because when media outlets use race as a template for discussing crime, the template takes the focus off the type of crime and places the listener's or viewer's attention on what type of person committed the crime. As a result of the racial template, we come to believe that the goal of fighting crime centers on defeating or

THE ART OF GOD

controlling those types of people (who commit crimes), rather than finding a way to eradicate the type of crimes committed by any and all perpetrators.

Let us consider some of the values that gang life can produce. I remember watching a television program on gangs recently. The program was a documentary and featured interviews with inmates who were serving time inside different jails. One professed gang member said that he had killed a childhood friend for being an informant. He also said that he went to the funeral knowing that he had killed the person inside the casket. Not only did he sit there comfortably through the service, but he did not feel any remorse for the killing the entire time. In his mind the "rat" betrayed his tribe, (a.k.a. his gang), and the rat got what he deserved. Misguided group loyalty can hinder one's ability to develop any empathy or compassion for those on the outside of the group. This results not only in dispassion but in a complete sense of detachment from the plight of others.

How many times has your reaction to a crime story been determined by the perpetrator's skin color? Have you ever, while watching a television piece about crime, felt glad that a convicted (white or black) perpetrator got what was deserved? "I am glad that they got what they deserved" is a typical response when the news of swift and harsh justice is about an "outsider." I want to caution you against being too quick to justify those feelings as simply normal. The inmate in the television program I mentioned above said on that program that he observed his victim's family grieving and felt nothing. Do we really want to be a people who feel nothing when we learn of the hardship of another who may not be part of our tribe?

Later on in the television interview, the inmate received news that his uncle had died. His uncle had been the only male figure to ever care about him. The news hit him so hard that he began to examine his past. The inmate's personal pain caused him to consider the pain that his murderous past had caused the extended family of his victims. Tragically he had never thought of his victim and the victim's family as people before; they had been simply an extension of the other: you know, "those people."

The Community of God

Choirs and gangs are two very different groups or wholes into which individuals organize themselves. I call the volunteer process that occurs when forming a choir *spontaneous organization*. First, the members become excited at the prospect of singing, and then they make the decision to join.

Gangs are populated through quite a different process. You are either recruited into them, or you undergo some type of initiation process before you are permitted to join. My friend Jerry Perez recently related a story to me about a time that he was recruited to join a gang in his neighborhood. The gang was called the Aces. Jerry was encouraged to get a tattoo that depicted a playing card, such as the ace of spades, on his arm. He said that his friends were very persistent in their recruitment until he informed them that the tattoo was a deal breaker. Jerry laughed when he recalled the eventual outcome. It appears the gang disbanded in a very short time, leaving many of his peers walking around with aces on their arms, which they no longer wanted. Choir and gang affiliations are transitory by definition because both will end at some future date. The use of racial categories to classify people has not been transitory, and exclusionary practices based on racial classification will not end until we all are willing to change our attitudes about what it means to be human. A healthy understanding of what constitutes a person should result in the ability to see value and worth in every piece of the art of God.

Gangs, tribes, choirs, nation-states, and even entire continents have something in common because they are all local to something. This means that the people who live within the boundaries of that particular area or group are really in, and the outsiders are really out. We then get a feeling of security or self-worth just by being *part of* that whatever. However, the God of the Bible is not a local God. God is not local to your race, your ethnic heritage, your denomination, or even your preferred style of worship. So what should that God's "locality" look like?

The community of God should exist to offer a place to any and all who would come; for that to happen, *all* must be made to feel that they are equal to and with each other, in order to be genuinely welcome. The openness necessary for creating this type of community will not come via church programs such as feeding the poor, taking mission trips, or having more minority speakers at denominational meetings before returning to isolation. It will only become reality with a commitment from church attenders to love and accept the other—a commitment that results in members' actually caring about the everyday circumstances that those "other people" are striving to overcome.

Two obvious and related questions are, what is love and how can we tell the authentic from the inauthentic? Just think how radical the biblical directive to "love your enemies" really is (Matthew 5:44). That command is not simply a suggestion to forgive or overlook perceived wrongs perpetrated against you. It is instruction for how to proactively love the people that you have, or your group has, identified as enemies for whatever reason. The sad truth is that loving the other is so unnatural to us that our instincts will lie to us and tell us that it is impossible to do. In our culture, "the self" rules, and we have convinced ourselves that we have no responsibility to be concerned about "the other." That means any other, and quite often that includes members of our immediate family.

There is a story in the Bible about two brothers named Cain and Abel. Cain murdered Abel, and it is assumed by many that he killed his brother in a fit of jealous rage. What is interesting about the story is the amount of violence that one brother was willing to foist upon the other. The Bible says that these two brothers were the first human beings born on earth, and Abel is the first to die. From the very beginning of our species, we have had the predisposition to do harm to "the other" that lives among us. We have developed many artificial theories and justifications to divert our attention away from one obvious conclusion: Given the choice either to live at peace with the other or to dominate the other through political, social, or physical violence, we have consistently chosen to dominate the other.

Jesus's dream, and his vision, for how we should live is quite different. He died for "his others" (us) rather than persecute or oppress them. He asks that each of us follow him down the same path of love and reconciliation towards the other. Today we live in a world where a great number of human beings are experiencing some form of oppression in their daily lives. Some put forward the belief that their struggles exist because they happen to live under oppressive political systems. Others speculate that their oppression could be a result of their lack of education and the accompanying limited opportunity. The misfortune of others is frequently written off as a consequence of bad luck, laziness, or poor choices. But do any of these reasons really matter? Does identifying a cause for human suffering give us the right to run away from the Christian imperative to extend love and compassion to those who are suffering? I think not.

In the Christian tradition every person living is a work of art created by a benevolent and loving God. Furthermore, the Christian tradition recognizes the inherent goodness of all that was created by the master artist, God. Open a Bible and read the following verses in the very first book; Genesis 1:4, 1:10, 1:12, 1:18, 1:21, 1:25, 1:31, and you will see that God said everything he created was indeed good. This means that God does not create abstract art, or art that is lesser in quality than the other pieces within creation. In fact every human being created by the artist named God is in some form a representation of the artist. Nothing that exists can be considered good or valuable apart from how it relates to God. All great art is simultaneously a matter of aesthetics and a matter of utility. When we apply the previous sentence to our discussion, it means that resident in every person is a degree of God's attribute of infinite beauty, running concurrently with the capacity for doing infinitely good things. What follows from this is that whenever any human being suffers poor treatment or neglect at the hands of another, a piece of God's art is being defiled and desecrated. This should not happen in the community of God. Each of us must commit to affirming the value and dignity of every individual by recognizing the spiritual nature of the community of God. The culture that exists in God's community is rooted in morality, justice, and a genuine desire for the best for others. The Danish philosopher Søren Kierkegaard shed further light on how we are to love "the others" in the community of God: "Forsake *all* distinctions so that you can love your neighbor."[32] As I close, please consider that each one of us is another's "other"! Each of us needs to make the effort to become better neighbors to *every* "other." A good first step would be to abandon the firmly rooted habit of judging the art of God solely by its external appearance.

"There can be no otherness only variation within the Art of God"

—Jimi Calhoun

3. Kierkegaard, *Works of Love*, 75.

Bibliography

Bach-Cantatas.com/. "Lorenz Christoph Mizler von Kolf," http://www.bach-cantatas.
com/Lib/Mizler-Lorenz-Christoph.htm/.

Bach-Cantatas.com/. "Guide to Bach Tour: Arnstadt," http://www.bach-cantatas.com/
Tour/Arnstadt.htm/.

Beck, Ulrich. *A God of One's Own: Religion's Capacity for Peace and Potential for Violence.*
Translated by Rodney Livingstone. Cambridge: Polity, 2010

Bennet, James B. *Religion and the Rise of Jim Crow in New Orleans.* Princeton: Princeton
University Press, 2005

Biography.com/ (Bio). "Louis Armstrong Biography," http://www.biography.com/people/
louis-armstrong-9188912#younger-years&/.

Britannica.com/. "Middle Ages," http://www.britannica.com/EBchecked/topic/380873/
Middle-Ages/.

Brown, Anthony, and Anthony Brown's Asian American Orchestra. *India & Africa: A
Tribute to John Coltrane.* Water Baby Records, 2010.

Buchholz, Elke Linda et al. *Art: A World History.* New York: Abrams, 2007.

Castlevechi, Davide. "Dante's Universe, and Ours." http://www.pbs.org/wgbh/nova/blogs/
physics/2012/07/dantes-universe/.

Carreras, Iris. "Christopher Lane, Australian Baseball Player, Killed by Bored Okla. Teens,
Police Say." *CBS News.* August 20, 2013, http://www.cbsnews.com/news/christopher-
lane-australian-baseball-player-killed-by-bored-okla-teens-police-say/.

Dictionary.com/. "Soundscape," http://dictionary.reference.com/browse/soundscape/

Giddins, Gary. *Celebrating Bird: The Triumph of Charlie Parker.* New York: Beech Tree,
1987

Gutman, Robert W. *Mozart: A Cultural Biography.* New York: Harcourt Brace, 1999.

Hanover Ensemble. *Music for Lord Abingdon.* MSR Classics MS 1099, 1 CD, program
notes on Johann Christian Bach et al. by John Solum, http://hanoverianfoundation.
org/Abingdon%20Page.html/.

Horn, Stacy. *Imperfect Harmony: Finding Happiness Singing with Others.* Chapel Hill, NC:
Algonquin, 2013

Jimmierodgers.com/. "Biography," http://www.jimmierodgers.com/

Johns, Cathryn, and Edwin Blake. "Cognitive Maps in Virtual Environments: Facilitation
of Learning through the Use of Innate Spatial Abilities." In Proceedings of the 1st

International Conference on Computer Graphics, Virtual Reality, and Visualisation, by AFRIGRAPH, 125–29. New York: ACM Press, 2001.

Kierkegaard, Søren. *Works of Love*. New York: Harper, 1964.

Ladd, George Eldon. *The Gospel of the Kingdom: Scripture Studies in the Kingdom of God*. Grand Rapids: Eerdmans, 1990.

Laszlo, Ervin. *Science and the Akashic Field: An Integral Theory of Everything*. 2nd ed. Rochester, VT: Inner Traditions, 2007.

Levitin, Daniel J. *This Is Your Brain on Music: The Science of a Human Obsession*. New York: Penguin, 2006

Lyricsplayground.com/. "Mama Don't Allow: Traditional," http://lyricsplayground.com/alpha/songs/m/mamadontallow.shtml/.

Margolick, David, "The Day Louis Armstrong Made Noise," New York Times, Septem-ber 23, 2007, http://www.nytimes.com/2007/09/23/opinion/23margolick.html?page-wanted=all&_r=0/.

Merida, Kevin, ed., and the staff of the *Washington Post*. *Being a Black Man: At the Corner of Progress and Peril*. Cambridge: Public Affairs, 2007.

Naxos.com/. "History of Classical Music," http://www.naxos.com/education/brief_history.asp/.

Nerburn, Kent. *Neither Wolf nor Dog: On Forgotten Roads with an Indian Elder*. Novato CA: New World Library, 2002

Nouwen, Henri J. M. *In the Name of Jesus: Reflections on Christian Leadership*. New York: Crossroad, 1989.

O'Donnell, Laurence. "Music and the Brain," http://www.cerebromente.org.br/n15/mente/musica.html/.

Porter, Lewis. *John Coltrane: His Life and Music*. Michigan American Music Series. Ann Arbor: University of Michigan Press, 1999.

Public Domain Songs. "Keep on the Sunny Side," http://www.pdinfo.com/PD-Song-List/PD-Song-List-Best-K.php/.

Rasmussen, Michelle. "Bach, Mozart, and the 'Musical Midwife,'" http://www.schillerinstitute.org/music/m_rasmus_801.html/.

ReformationSA.org/. "Johann Sebastian Bach," http://www.reformationsa.org/index.php/history/90-johann-sebastian-bach/.

Rosen, Charles. *The Classical Style: Haydn, Mozart, Beethoven*. Expanded ed. New York: Norton, 1998.

Shipton, Alyn. *A New History of Jazz*. London: Continuum, 2001.

Shonberg, Harold C. *The Lives of the Great Composers*. 3rd ed. New York: Norton, 1997.

Spears, Richard A. *McGraw-Hill's Dictionary of American Slang and Colloquial Expressions*. 4th ed. New York: McGraw-Hill, 2006.

Stevens, Patsy. "Ludwig von Beethoven," http://gardenofpraise.com/ibdbeet.htm/.

Stocker, Abbey. "The Craziest Statistic You'll Read about North American Missions," *Christianity Today Online*, August 9, 2013, http://www.christianitytoday.com/ct/2013/august-web-only/non-christians-who-dont-know-christians.html/.

Vedantam, Shankar. "How to Win That Music Competition? Send a Video." Feature on National Public Radio, *Morning Edition*, August 20, 2013, http://www.npr.org/2013/08/20/213551358/how-to-win-that-music-competition-send-a-video/.

Volf, Miraslov. *Allah: A Christian Response*. New York: HarperOne, 2011

Volf, Miraslov, and William Katerberg, eds. *The Future of Hope: Christian Tradition amid Modernity and Postmodernity*. Grand Rapids: Eerdmans, 2004.

Watkins, Tom et al. "Baby Shot Dead in Stroller; Two Georgia Teens Charged with Murder." *CNN*, March 23, 2013, http://www.cnn.com/2013/03/22/US/GEORGIA-BABY-KILLED/.

Wikipedia. "Appalachia," http://en.wikipedia.org/wiki/Appalachia/.

Wikipedia. "Die Entführung aus dem Serail," Wolfgang Amadeus Mozart. http://en.wikipedia.org/wiki/Die_Entführung_aus_dem _Serail/.

Wikipedia. "Jazz," http://en.wikipedia.org/wiki/Jazz/.

Wikiperdia. "Meme," http://en.wikipedia.org/wiki/Meme/.

Wikipedia. "Storyville," http://en.wikipedia.org/wiki/Storyville,_New_Orleans/.

Wikiquote. "The Picture of Dorian Gray," http://en.wikiquote.org/wiki/The_Picture_of_Dorian_Gray/.

Wikiquote. "Perseverance," Walter Elliott, in *The Spiritual Life: Doctrine and Practice of Christian Perfection* (1918), http://en.wikiquote.org/wiki/Perseverance/.

Wikiquote. "Walt Whitman," http://en.wikiquote.org/wiki/Walt_Whitman/.

Wilde, Oscar. "All Art Is Useless," http://www.brainyquote.com/quotes/quotes/o/oscarwilde161961.htm/.

Yetman, Norman R. *Voices from Slavery: 100 Authentic Slave Narratives*. Mineola NY: Dover, 1999.